Making Kin Not Population

Making Kin Not Population

Edited by Adele E. Clarke and Donna Haraway

PRICKLY PARADIGM PRESS
CHICAGO

Prickly Paradigm Press, LLC
5629 South University Avenue
Chicago, IL 60637

www.prickly-paradigm.com

ISBN: 9780996635561
LCCN: 2018941392

Printed in the United States of America on acid-free paper.

Contents

Note from the editors:

Prickly Paradigm Press publishes short interventions in current debates aimed at provoking broader engagement with the issues. The main ideas and references for *Making Kin Not Population* appear in this book. Our "Sourcenotes" with further discussion and extended referencing to sources appear only online and can be downloaded as PDFs. Beginning with a short quote from the paragraph to which they refer, Sourcenotes are listed by the page of this booklet on which an endnote would have appeared. The full references for the book are also online and downloadable for ease of access to the websites listed. For full citation information, please go to http://www.prickly-paradigm.com/titles/Making-Kin-not-Population.html.

Introducing
Making Kin Not Population

Adele E. Clarke

Our intervention *Making Kin Not Population* centers on generating feminist science studies-informed pro-kin *and* non-natalist politics of reproductive justice for *all* species and future imaginaries toward their realization in our era of environmental crises and degradation. Human-related and human-caused burdens on the planet, including both our expanding numbers and devastatingly extractive, unjust practices of living and dying, are immensely corrosive and destructive of too many human and nonhuman ways of life.

In 1900, world population is estimated to have been 1.6 billion people; today it stands at c7.6 billion and is estimated to exceed c11 billion people by 2100, if birth rates continue to drop as they have been almost everywhere. For human survival, food production will need to increase considerably, affecting ecologies and biodiversity even more devastatingly. These burdens are far too great, too structural, and too ruinous for feminists and our allies to ignore any longer, however fraught addressing them may be. Multispecies reproductive justice fully integrated with human and nonhuman environmental justice and savvy environmental action is our goal; making kin, especially non-biological kin, is our fundamental means.

We seek to bring feminism, reproductive justice, environmentalism and environmental justice together while *simultaneously disengaging* from ongoing colonizing frames of knowledge and practices, including assumptions of human exceptionalism and the separation of humans from nature. As progressive feminists, we have long opposed policies and practices of population control—by which we mean *the use of any means of coercion* of people regarding their reproductive lives and futures—as anathema to feminist reproductive rights and justice. Challengingly, at the same time, we are concerned about the impacts and consequences of expanding numbers of humans on the planet. As Crist, Mora and Engelman recently argued in *Science*, "An important approach to sustaining biodiversity and human well-being is through actions that can slow and eventually reverse population growth: investing in universal access to reproductive health services and contraceptive technologies, advancing women's education, and achieving gender equality." Such interventions are, however, neither simple nor unproblematic.

"Making kin" non-biologically is urgently part of this endeavor. We need to generate new kin inventions, new concepts and practices for making kith and kindred, as well as attending and attuning to how people and peoples *already* make and value other-than-biogenetic kin in non-imperialist ways. Such alternatives need to be *increasingly accessible and legitimate across diverse cultures and nation states.* Sahlins' recent book on kinship transculturally asserts that people become kin largely by sharing experiences and generating a sense of belonging. Kinfolk are parts of one another to the extent that what happens to one is *felt* by the other, such that we live each other's lives and die each other's deaths. *Biological* connection is not requisite. Valuing such "belonging" as much as—perhaps more than—"blood relation" is what we are urging in *Making Kin Not Population*. Moreover, and deeply important here, such belonging—such kinship—can not only be across species but blur such boundaries. The human/nonhuman binary is a distinction that many beings on this planet do not make, instead seeing and sensing continuities of being through non-Enlightenment, non-secular approaches to understanding such as Indigenous cosmopolitanism, religions, or spiritualities.

We are well aware that all our major categories immediately signal trouble: *feminism, reproduction, population, environment, kin.* All are what Williams called *keywords* and we cannot ignore the problems and complications these categories pose—singly much less in ever-morphing combinations! But they also collect energies for making kin otherwise—toward generating serious strategies toward reproductive justice across species, enhancing environmental protections, and stemming the ongoing loss of biodiversity. These problematic categories situate important roots of our discussion. All the authors here have been involved and implicated in these issues for decades. We seek to move conversations and action in new, speculative and more hopeful directions that can elaborate strategies and diversify kinmaking.

First, some background. In spring 2013, Donna Haraway and I spoke at separate feminist academic events at the same university, each raising issues engaged here, but unaware of the other's concerns. A woman who attended both talks told me of Donna's comments, noting that both our remarks were met with what Donna later called a "booming silence." Breaking that silence with each other, we decided to organize a session on these fraught issues, held at the 2015 meetings of the Society for Social Studies of Science which has long welcomed feminist interventions. Our abstract for that session, our first collaborative response to the "booming silence," provocatively framed its loose bases as follows:

> Feminist STS scholarship has long and richly addressed biogenetic reproduction, focusing on race, region, sexuality, class, gender, and more. However, feminist STS has also largely been silent about reducing the human burden on earth while strengthening ecojustice for people and other critters as means and not just ends. Can we develop anti-colonial, anti-imperialist, anti-racist, STS-informed feminist politics of peopling the earth in current times, when babies should be rare yet precious and real pro-family and community politics for young and old remain rare yet urgently needed? How can we develop collaborative politics recognizing that peoples subjected to (ongoing) genocides may need more children? How can we intervene in the relentless glut of attention devoted to problematic, costly "rights" and "needs" for (mainly richer) women to have babies as an individual "choice"?
>
> **Questions**: How to nurture durable multi-generational non-biological kin-making, while humans everywhere transition to vastly less reproduction? What alternative ways of flourishing can be nurtured

*across generations and across cultures, religions,
nations? How to deter on-going anti-feminist population control efforts while generating innovative
discourses that legitimate non-natalist policies and
choices? How to promote research on forms of contraception women and men want (and can use under
diverse circumstances) and reproductive services that
actually serve? How to build non-natalist kin-making
technologies and sciences in housing, travel, urban
design, food growing, environmental rehabilitation,
etc.?*

*Where are the feminist utopian, collaborative,
risky imaginings and actions for earthlings in a
mortal, damaged, human-heavy world? Why hasn't
feminist STS taken the lead in such fundamental
endeavors?*

Our session had a "standing-room-only" attendance of
about two hundred, and generated intense and
provocative discussion of many issues. The panel therefore decided to pursue this booklet based on our talks
as our next collaborative effort to address "the booming silence."

Intensifying Urgencies

Since we began this shared undertaking, many events have dramatically underscored its need, including:

- Much greater international recognition of the profound problems caused by climate change by individuals as well as organizations, states and nation-states, many now increasingly committed to seeking effective policies for responsibly reducing its human-related causes. "To pretend that it's such a tragedy is to pretend that there's no social and collective responsibility for the outcome." Responsibility and accountability echo loudly here;

- Ferguson and all the related horrific racist murders—Tamir Rice, Sandra Bland, Michael Brown, Ayana Jones, Eric Garner, John Crawford, Walter Scott, Eric Harris, say their names—and injustices before and since, as well as persistently high rates of Black infant mortality and reproductive injustice that have led to transnational insistence that Black Lives Matter. Incisively analyzed by Angela Davis and Keeanga Taylor, these issues and their links to environmental racism are taken up here especially by Ruha Benjamin;

- The same murderous injustices have long occurred in Indigenous communities and in other communities of color. In 2016, the Standing Rock Sioux whose lands and waters are seriously threatened and others defended the site of the proposed crossing of the Cannonball River against the Dakota Access Keystone XL pipeline for many months. They asserted that prolonged *environmental degradation is multigenerational Indigenous reproductive injustice*, discussed in this booklet by Kim TallBear and Michelle Murphy;

- China repealed its one-child policy for an official two-child policy, accompanied by a resurgence of often nationalist pronatalisms from the US to Europe to Turkey to Cuba to Asian countries that had profoundly reduced their rates of reproduction through policy and service initiatives (some coercive). These issues are engaged here by Yu-ling Huang and Chia-ling Wu, including innovative feminist policy alternatives;

- Sterilization abuse, a particularly vicious form of population control and reproductive violence, continues—still especially but not only among poor people of color. A 2014 case of such "medical homicide" occurred in India when 13 women being paid to be sterilized died in a mass camp organized by village "motivators" themselves paid "by the head." In California, over a quarter of all sterilizing tubal ligations done on women prisoners from 2005 to 2013 were performed illegally—without their written consent; in Tennessee, some prisoners can now "choose" jail time or sterilization;

- Millions of desperate people continue to risk life and limb in hopes of relocating from endless war zones and/or places rendered economically untenable often by climate change-induced droughts, floods, and famines to places where living less precariously might, just might, be possible. In 2015, according to the UN, "The number of international migrants—persons living in a country other than where they were born—reached 244 million for the world as a whole, *a 41 per cent increase compared to 2000...* This figure includes almost 20 *million* refugees";

- Women's access to abortion has dramatically decreased, and its legality is currently in peril in many places. In 2017, the Trump administration also terminated US funding of the United Nations Population Fund, a transnational provider and supporter of family planning services, including contraception but not abortion, to women in at least 155 countries. *Contraception too* is now under siege as part of the Republican "war against women," engendering international resistance and alternative funding strategies;

- Taiwan's feminist woman President Tsai Ing-wen issued a formal apology to aboriginal Taiwanese people for centuries of "pain and mistreatment," drawing attention to the nation's destructive use of one of their homelands, Orchid Island, as a depository for nuclear waste. Such ecological trespasses on native lands are transnational issues for Indigenous peoples with reproductive consequences, addressed here by Ruha Benjamin, Michelle Murphy and Kim TallBear;

- Across the globe, various forms of neo-fascism, right-wing anti-immigration and antifeminist white supremacy are on the rise as are various forms of ethnic cleansing, with dictatorial world leaders imperiling democracy, the environment, and women's lives alike.

There are, of course, many more such issues.

David Hess has drawn our attention to "undone science"—research *not* pursued largely because it is unprofitable or "too" political. But there are also *undone feminist politics and biopolitics* which now lead us to ask: Why haven't the issues of warped distributions of resources and densities of human beings in conditions of structural injustice and forced displacement been systematically examined by more feminists as fundamental, *including* the question of increasing numbers of people? Why *hasn't* the issue of too many people on the planet, especially in relation to climate change and other environmental catastrophes from Big Agriculture to Big Pharma concerns, already become a *major* feminist concern—both inside and outside the academy?

As feminists, we are not alone in raising these issues and an array of recent examples is discussed below. However, such engagements remain thin on the ground compared to feminist pursuits of IVF, surrogacy, and related natalist projects. We therefore ask, are (many? most?) contemporary feminism(s) and feminist science studies *tacitly* pronatalist? Are feminists and STS scholars actively afraid of engaging these issues of human numbers, environment, and population control, with all their complexities and difficult histories? There are, for example, many grave problems with the (over)loaded concept of "population," engaged vividly in this volume (see especially chapters by

Murphy and Haraway). What *are* the alternatives? How can we discuss such thorny problems and articulate new positions in ways that are *also* respectfully pro-mother, pro-child, pro-parent and pro-person?

But first let us situate the broad project of *Making Kin* a bit more historically.

Situating *Making Kin*:
Feminism, Reproduction, Demography/Population, Environment

The key backdrops for *Making Kin* are feminist activism and scholarship focused on three domains: reproduction, demography/population, and the environment. Each consists in strong, diverse and increasingly transnational social movement organizations initiated during or prior to the early 20th century: 1) the largely liberal to progressive feminist birth control, abortion and (later) related reproductive rights and justice movements; 2) the largely conservative population, demography and population control movements; and 3) a wide variety of more, less, and non-feminist conservation, environmental, and environmental justice movements. Their mutual influences, antipathies, overlaps, and overlapping alliances have become increasingly manifest and complex in the 21st century.

Shaping these movements and their relations are several overarching and interlocking motifs: Moore's Capitalocene "world-ecologies" historically undergirded by colonial annihilation of Indigenous peoples, Haraway's Plantationocene epoch of enslaved human, animal, and plant life for extractive purposes, and post-WWII, what Murphy calls "the economization of life," discussed next.

Capitalocene and Plantationocene World-Ecologies

The "Anthropocene" is one proposed name for our current geological age as the historical epoch of our planet during which *human activity has become the dominant influence on climate, environment, geology and ecosystems*. Various "start dates" are debated, ranging from 1610 as the beginning of depopulation of the Americas by colonization and genocide through European conquest, to August 6, 1945 when the first nuclear bomb was exploded by the US over Hiroshima, demonstrating the extent of humans' destructive capacities, to the "Great Acceleration" of mass extinctions and environmental devastation post-WWII.

However, the concept of the Anthropocene *per se* has been challenged due to both its presentation of humanity as "a homogeneous acting unit" without *any* analysis of highly differential power relations among us, *and* for reinstalling the primacy of *Homo sapiens* over all other life forms—the hubris of its human-centeredness. Moore has offered the more compelling alternative of the "Capitalocene" since it was the rise of capitalism post 1450 that has most profoundly altered the relations of humans with the rest of nature since the rise of agriculture.

Moore asserts that *Capitalocene modernity is a capitalist world-ecology premised on specific exploitative and extractive configurations of humanity-in-nature.* Crucial here, inside this logic of capitalist modernity, the market, production, political, and cultural relations are reduced to "social" relations, while Nature is segmented off and (mis)conceptualized as "natural"— *as independent of and separate from humans.* This framing thereby legitimates the appropriation of "Cheap Nature" throughout the Capitalocene epoch. Moreover, it legitimates the "enclosure of the atmosphere" as a gigantic dumping ground for greenhouse gases and other industrial and agribusiness debris and garbage—"wastelanding" or the creation of "sacrificial zones."

For Moore, "Capitalism is not an economic system; it is not a social system; it is *a way of organizing nature....* This is capitalism *as a project.*" Today, the depletion and demise of "Cheap Nature" on which the Capitalocene has relied is repeatedly demonstrated to us by increasingly frequent weather and environmental catastrophes—climate change writ larger and larger and larger. To Moore and others, this *signals the breakdown of the strategies and relations that have sustained capital accumulation for over five centuries,* a momentous process.

With appreciation of Moore's Capitalocene intervention, Haraway provides considerably more feminist perspectives and concepts to capture these major shifts. Begun in colonial eras across the globe post c1492, plantations of many kinds largely based on slave labor were designed to create and sustain production of the scope of wealth related to the extractable profits and relentless growth of capital. Haraway calls this the "Plantationocene" epoch to signal more clearly *the earth-changing patterns of forced life, forced death and mass transportation of peoples (usually as slaves), plants, and animals* in radical and destructive simplifications of extant eco-worlds. Moreover, as Haraway notes, in shifting forms, the Plantationocene is still with us (e.g., in oil palm and coffee plantations, and mono-cropping more generally), still dependent on quasi-slave relations.

The Plantationocene epoch makes particular sense to us as it takes into account Winant's argument that:

> Race was invented along with the modern era. It was central to the liftoff of capitalism…. *Indigenous deaths* in the Americas in the first century of European rule totaled c. 42 million/*80% of the total [population]*…Deaths directly attributable to the Atlantic slave trade…: 8-10 million in Africa…; *10-12 million in the "middle passage"*; and 5 million in Jamaican "seasoning" camps alone.

These figures make the Plantationocene all too palpable. As Winant notes, slavery was among the first international businesses.

Another refinement of focus within the Anthropocene/Capitalocene/Plantationocene debates is attention to what Steffen and colleagues call the "Great Acceleration," the post-WWII and Cold War eras when "changes simultaneously sweeping across the socio-economic and biophysical spheres of the Earth System" effected "the *most rapid transformation of the human relationship with the natural world in the history of humankind*," including mass extinctions. Ebron and Tsing further "argue that the peculiar configuration of class, race, and gender in the United States during this period played a major role…. Contingent US developments shaped global trajectories." Transnational economic development policies, including the implementation of population control, were a primary means. For feminists and some others, "Uncovering the *intersectional inequalities of the Great Acceleration* helps" clarify those highly raced and gendered politics.

The Economization of Life

In Murphy's framework of the "economization of life," a new imaginary of "population" as a problematic emerged in the early 19th century. It later coalesced in mid-20th-century economic theory through the use of "population control" policies post WWII as key tools of economic development. In short, Malthusian and related eugenic race science and racial population goals blatantly framed in the 19th century were more subtly reframed in the mid-20th century as *selective* national goals for engendering economic prosperity through calibrated population "adjustments." These were/are to be achieved largely via national population control policies, strategies, programs and technologies themselves inscribed especially on—and into—women's bodies, including coercively. With other feminist works such as Ginsberg and Rapp's, the economization of life again places reproduction at the heart of social, economic, and political theory.

Key here for Murphy and for us, *at this scale of conceptualization, living human beings recede from view, rendering "population" itself as an experimental object (lab rat, guinea pig) in need of governance.* It is against this de-humanized "thingness" of "population" and population control that distinctively *feminist* reproductive and environmental activism and scholarship must be understood. The economization of life is a vivid example of "a 'social' science emphasizing 'prediction' and 'control' [that] can too easily use the veil of 'objectivity' to hide a dehumanizing impulse." Or, as Amade M'charek stated, "The factness of facts depends on their ability to disconnect themselves from the practices that helped produce them."

Murphy further argued:

> [The concept of] population reinvigorated temporalized logics of *modern* and *backward*, giving *an economic alibi*, and new lease, on old evolutionary hierarchies of human worth, …human waste, human surplus, unproductive life, and life in excess of economic value…[F]ertility was a pivotal focus…. Thus the *measures of economized life* could underwrite violent, coercive, and racist projects, as much as foster voluntary or even feminist ones…

The logics and the means of measurement of the economization of life continue to be lively in theories and practices across disciplines, including social *and* natural sciences. It is also not accidental that the framework of the economization of life was reworked post WWII, the historical moment when many former colonies became supposedly autonomous nation states. Frameworks of the economization of life offered new forms of neo-colonial governance promotable by more powerful nation states, typically conceptualized as "development."

Capitalocene and Plantationocene "world-ecologies" and the profoundly enmeshed practices of the "economization of life" speeded up through the "Great Acceleration" together set the scene for our present moment. Notably, for many people in the global South and in extremely poor parts of the global North, these conditions have long been systemic and chronic. Today the global nature of global warming and the Capitalocene are distributing the damages in less stratified ways, including across the global North.

What is to be done? Turning an important corner not towards a fantasized edenic future but attending to possibilities of alternative ways of living

and being on this planet—including feminist—
Haraway offers what she calls the "Chthulucene" as a
possible current epoch. The Chthulucene is "a time-
place for learning to stay with the trouble of living and
dying in response-ability on a damaged earth."
Haraway's Chthulucene pays care-full attention in the
here and now to the enmeshed webs of multi-species
living and being. It asks how the broadest kinds of
accountabilities can be brought into play, especially
through generating, maintaining and valuing *kinships
and other mutualities that go far beyond the biogenetic.*
Instead of abandoning all hope with often masculinist-
driven claims that it is already "too late for planet
Earth," the Chthulucene is about trying to take
responsibility, *transpecies* strategies for "staying with
the trouble" we humans have made. It is about joining
in the ongoingness of life *now* with feminist modes of
caring about and for a planet sorely in need of attention
(discussed further in her chapter).

Haraway's Chthulucene is one response, one
pathway among many emergent alternatives discussed
in this booklet toward more ethical ways of refusing the
premises of the Capitalocene, the Plantationocene, and
the economization of life. Instead the goal becomes
taking more profound responsibility for environmental
degradation and mass extinctions, and struggling to
make and value heterogeneous kin towards multispecies reproductive justice.

Making Kin:
Prior Progressive Feminist Efforts

To remind us how diversely *progressive feminists* have previously taken up issues of reproduction, demography/population, and environment, I offer here some remembrances of things past and, in the next section, some examples of current feminist engagements.

In 1970, early in second wave feminism, Shulamith Firestone's *The Dialectic of Sex* appeared, reinterpreting "Marx, Engels and Freud to make a case that a 'sexual class system' [runs] deeper than any other social or economic divide. For Firestone, the traditional family structure...*was at the core of women's oppression.*" In Firestone's own words: "[U]ntil the decision not to have children or not to have them 'naturally' is *at least as legitimate* as traditional childbearing, women are as good as forced into their female roles."

Firestone's solutions to end the oppression of women in childbearing and rearing drew deeply upon feminist techno-social alternatives—artificial wombs and shared upbringing of those children by people who wanted to do so regardless of blood relation. For Firestone, *alternative means of making kin should be available (never required), along with enhanced legitimacy for not having biological children.*

Distinctively resonating here, Firestone's fascinating chapter on "Feminism and Ecology" viewed population as "a genuine ecological problem." In Sarah Franklin's recent reappraisal, it was "the key issue linking feminist concerns to revolutionary ecology (then in its infancy...)," tying "current threats to the human species (pollution, famine, overcrowding, etc.)

and the degraded status of the female of the species."
Most of all, Firestone wondered why population issues
were "*so consistently ignored*" by feminists.

Significantly, as Franklin underscores,
Firestone's progressive biofuturist vision *was premised
on a revolution in gender roles having occurred*: "In
Firestone's dialectic of...reprotech..., it is *the revolutionary capacity of technological progress* that establishes
the crucial link between feminism, population control,
and ecological sustainability." With foreboding,
Firestone had written, "to envision [technologies of
population control and fertility enhancement] in the
hands of the present powers is to envision a nightmare."
Today, in the absence of such a revolution—made
vividly clear by #MeToo and *The Handmaid's Tale*—
Firestone's nightmare is very much with us. Coercive
population control continues, fertility enhancement
proliferates, and gender roles and gendered reproductive differences intensify, though they also generate
resistance.

Superficial readings by some feminists and
others led to Firestone's work being partialized, carica-
tured and dismissed as "feminist folly." But rereading
Firestone today, too much seems prescient—especially
her insights on links between human numbers, structural domination of women (largely through lack of
economic options), and environmental degradation.
Reading Firestone and Franklin together also made me
wonder whether the absence of a full-scale revolution in
gender roles ultimately best "explains" the "booming
silence" that initiated our efforts in this booklet, and
whether, by advocating "making kin not population,"
we will invoke similar disdain, feminist and otherwise.

In contrast with Firestone, other second wave
feminist framings of reproduction were broad, inclusive,

ambitious and distinctively community-focused—
fundamentally about bringing new generations into the
world under sustaining local conditions for nurturance
in which they might not only survive but flourish.
Especially but not only in the writings and activisms of
women of color, reproductive theorizing involved housing, what is now called food security, violence prevention and treatment, prison reform, community involvement, etc., *as well as* full access to health care and
medical (including reproductive) technologies. Key
contributors included Cellestine Ware, Carol Stack,
Angela Davis and Patricia Hill Collins.

Particularly significant here, the ability to raise
the children one has, and raise them well, was and
remains an elusive goal for many women. Feminist
reproductive frameworks need to be broad and ambitious to *actively work against* the relentless "demeaning
of the reproduction of the poor," of the poor," North,
South, everywhere, as Khiari Bridges has noted. In our
view, making kin today again demands that similar
enlarged, ambitious and risk-taking approaches be
articulated and pursued under and taking into account
ever more desperate environmental conditions.

In 1990 as the third wave of feminism began,
Elaine Rapping wrote on "The Future of Motherhood"
in the *Socialist Feminist Reader*. She traced American
left feminist positionalities on reproductive issues—
from Firestone through "new reproductive technologies" (NRTs) and the emergence of FINRRAGE (the
Feminist International Network of Resistance to
Reproductive and Genetic Engineering), an international activist network centered on the dangers of NRTs
for women and their bodies.

Rapping argued that in the 1980s, the *cause
celebre* Baby M case of a surrogate mother refusing to

give up "her" baby had raised grave issues for many progressive feminists:

> It demonstrated how socialist analysis of class and race bias can lead to an equally crucial *retreat* from an equally crucial socialist-feminist tenet: that motherhood is *socially, not biologically,* constructed.... A number of feminists—liberal, radical, *and* socialist— were suddenly arguing as vehemently *for* the rights of the *biological* mother...as they had once argued for the right *not* to mother...

Biological mothering and motherhood again, as in first wave feminism, became core issues late in the second wave. Rapping continued presciently:

> In a post-Reagan world, where so much has been taken from us and so much that we dreamed of twenty years ago has not materialized, we must at all costs hang on to the two things we can still hope to own and control, our bodies and our biological offspring. And yet...[this is] fraught with political blind spots and contradictions.

Who—which women and which mothers—get to own and control their bodies and their children was and remains very highly stratified by class and race as Colen, Hill Collins, Richie, and many others have since argued. Making kin must thus confront the intensely racialized and classed (among other) dynamics that have largely defined reproductive control by privileging whiteness.

In the US, early/mid-20th-century birth control movements were largely white and liberal, as were the later abortion rights movements that led to abortion legalization in 1973. Starting in the 1970s, *progressive* feminist analyses of abortion rights and the "right to choose" led to a schism within feminism.

Liberal feminists remained focused on a politics of individualized choice and "abortion rights," resisting more social and stratified analyses of reproductive issues.

In sharp contrast, progressive feminist reproductive politics coalesced into what became known as "reproductive rights," also largely white, but significantly integrating analyses of race, class, etc. in early forms of intersectional thinking. These analyses led to activist organizing efforts against sterilization abuse and population control both of which, then as now, selectively targeted poor women of color and Indigenous women. An array of progressive, actively anti-racist feminist organizations emerged, including race/ethnicity specific groups. They also advocated for varied local community-focused parenting concerns, abortion rights and broad access to all reproductive health services. *Significant here, progressive feminists have grasped these politics at least since the 1970s.*

However, since the late 1970s, in the media and popular culture it has been "pro-choice" which received top billing in the requisite US political binary form, pitted against a growing array of right-wing "anti-abortion" and fetal "right to life" organizations and political platforms. Mol bitingly described "choice" as a rhetorical magic wand used to transform subordinated objects into self-determining subjects—*without* any corresponding changes in concrete, stratified practices that too often make "choice" a mockery at best. Underscoring these issues, Murphy further analyzed the stratifying consequences of the "whiteness" of early feminist self-help and other movements for feminist reproductive politics more broadly, noting how *biomedical* choice projects easily bleed into heightened liberal individualized politics of *consumer* choice still very much happening—and further stratifying—today.

Feminist *reproductive rights* advocates with their broader agendas had some superficial successes on national and international stages, notably the Cairo "consensus" at the 1994 International Conference on Population and Development where empowering women, especially through education, was deemed more effective long term than (often coercive) population control strategies. Yet in practice, the broader reproductive rights agendas long promoted by progressive feminists were largely displaced and ignored.

Post Cairo in the early 1990s, this provoked the rise, led especially by feminists of color, of *reproductive justice* movements, elaborating rapidly today. The continued emptiness of individualized "choice" politics for many if not most women globally, especially poor women of color and Indigenous women, has increasingly come under fire from reproductive justice scholars and activists transnationally. Instead, Shellee Colen's concept of "stratified reproduction" has become a key progressive feminist theoretical intervention. This concept allows and encourages further analysis of the *specific intersectionalities of race, class, gender and reproductive concerns with racist and economics-driven population control agendas.*. The questions become: *Which* women are encouraged to reproduce? *Which* women are discouraged from reproducing? Under what conditions?

The answers to those questions have largely reflected what Murphy calls the "economization of life." Reproduction is always and relentlessly individual *and* social *and* biological *and* cultural *and* political in complexly entangled ways. Grasping this, progressive feminist theorizing and research about reproduction has continued to proliferate. A major wing focuses on sustaining and extending the sadly still crucial long-standing feminist critiques of population control ideologies, policies, and practices. Recent work here offers deeper and more focused histories of population control projects in China, Taiwan, South Korea, India, Puerto Rico, Haiti, and other non-Western and Indigenous sites.

A new wave of progressive feminist research is concerned with *pronatal*, usually nationalist policies seeking to address dwindling populations of particular ethnic/racial composition, such as the proclaimed "demographic emergencies" of "not enough of the right kind of people" in Italy, Denmark, Turkey, Japan, Taiwan, and most recently asserted by US Republican leaders. Feminist and related critical progressive analyses of demography qua "science" have also been mounted, and proposals for alternatives offered. Yu-ling Huang and Chia-ling Wu (this volume) focus precisely on these issues in East Asia.

Since c1995, feminist STS scholarship combining insights of science and technology studies with those of feminist theory and research on reproductive, population and environmental topics, has exploded. For example, contraceptive technology *development* has long occurred at intersections of feminist birth control and (non- or anti-feminist) population control worlds, engendering the feminist distinction between "woman-controlled" versus "imposable" contraceptive technologies amenable to coercive use (e.g., IUDs, injectibles, and insertables, not under the woman user's direct control). What I termed "imposables" are today known more generally as "Long Acting Reversible Contraceptives" (LARCs). Used transnationally in population control programs since the 1950s, R&D on imposables/LARCs has been especially well funded, and their removal continues to be dangerous, costly and often difficult to access. In the US, coercion about LARCs has become so wide-spread that in 2016 SisterSong and the National Women's Health Network, feminist women's health groups, jointly developed a Statement of Principles regarding providing them.

Over five *million* "test tube babies" have now been born, accompanied by vast waves of feminist research on infertility, IVF, surrogacy, and related technological means of having babies, from sperm banks to "mitochondrial transfer" (also known as "three parent babies"), some pursued as feminist STS projects and some not. Such work is increasingly transnational, as is reproductive tourism to accomplish various goals. Segments of the biotechnology, regenerative medicine and global pharmaceutical industries also actively pursue *reproductive tissue* for various purposes. IVF, egg donation, sperm banks, and surrogacy have all become transnationally organized for-profit industries and sites of considerable feminist and ethical debate. In response, FINRRAGE concerns about negative consequences of various technologies for women's bodies and women's struggles for enhanced autonomy over their own lives have been reignited. The terrain of "critical kinship studies" has also been limned by Krolokke and colleagues.

Progressive feminist critiques of such reproductive issues, echoing earlier debates, center on several key points. First, contraception and abortion technologies are generally framed in terms of women's (and sometimes men's) *individual rights*, "choices," and families' reproductive situations. For progressive feminists, such individualized analytics are non-innocent; they *actively obscure structural conditions*, especially those linked to race, class, sexuality, gender identity, and place (both in the US and internationally), that may not only constrain "choice" but also exert subtle and blatant forms of coercion and abet further stratification of reproduction. Moreover, individualized analytics also obscure, à la Foucault and Murphy, *collective* practices of population management in terms of eugenics, nationalist pronatalism, neocolonialism, population control and their consequences. In short, individualized discourses make *biopolitics* politically invisible.

Second, as progressive feminists point out, the same analytics that actively *obscure* the dynamics of race, class, place, culture and history are now lively in rhetorics surrounding IVF, egg sourcing for research, cloning and the "new genetics." For example, Greenhalgh has argued that (feminist and other) STS-focused work on such topics too often present a familiar *Eurocentric* "biopolitical story...[O]n a more inclusive map of the world the politics of population governance remains an essential terrain of the politics of life." Moreover, feminist reproductive politics need to be further reconceptualized beyond North–South binaries, and to envision *futures generated* in "Southern" and other settings, as well as *imagined communities including other species and ecologies.* Global North/South feminist collaborations are taking the initiative.

Third are fundamental issues about how we conceptualize and study reproductive phenomena. In *Seizing the Means of Reproduction*, Murphy challenges framing such phenomena as events and instead asserts, "Reproduction is not so much a 'thing' as an overdetermined and distributed *process* that divergently brings individual lives, kinship, laboratories, race, nations, biotechnology, time, and affects into confluence." Others also emphasize the *processual* nature and fluidities of reproduction noting, however, that even feminist scholarship is very much "siloed" into research on *events* such as pregnancy and birth, contraception and abortion, etc. *Progressive feminist biopolitical theorizing does not flow or flourish across siloed research worlds.* Again, reproduction is always and relentlessly simultaneously individual, social, biological, cultural, and political—as well as environmental.

Making Kin:
Contemporary Feminist Engagements

So where are we now? The activism and scholarship discussed in this section selectively illustrate contemporary *simultaneous* feminist engagements with environmental, reproductive and demographic issues, which have rarely been pursued together in the past. While environmental issues have never lain dormant in feminist activism and scholarship around reproduction and population, climate change, global warming, mass extinctions, habitat destruction, recurrent famines, and diverse naturalcultural disasters have recently repositioned them more centrally. Heightened practices of caring for both human and nonhuman beings in entangled lives have surged in importance. But the politics— *including the feminist politics especially as these relate to race and class*—are complex and quite fraught.

For example, since 1991, the Committee on Women, Population and the Environment (CWPE) has investigated "the reasons why a variety of environmental, social, and security issues are defined or presented as *population* problems." Unlike many contributors to *Making Kin*, they do *not* believe that human numbers on the planet are linked to climate change and environmental degradation. The CWPE thus sustains earlier progressive feminist anti-population control positions, innovatively extending them through recent analyses of environmental problems by Silliman, King and others. In accord with many CWPE arguments, *Making Kin* contributors continue to very strongly oppose population control. But some of us are also attempting to position ourselves differently as progressive feminists vis-à-vis climate change and human impacts on the planet. As Ebron and Tsing note, this is a challenging new area of feminist discussion.

Another generative intersection is between environmental justice and reproductive justice movements and related concerns. Sasser studied this intersection vis-à-vis global health and development in US policy-making. What she found, *fully half a century* after second-wave feminists began loudly objecting to population control, was that still today in policy discourse, women are "reduced to intervenable subjects—a universal 'Woman'…[and] arguments rooted in Neo-Malthusian logic bubbled from [policy makers'] lips."

In refreshingly new and different ways, ethical issues regarding reproduction in relation to the natural world are being raised by varied feminist activists and scholars. The Conceivable Future project is a women-led network of Americans bringing awareness of the threats climate change poses to reproductive justice, and demanding an end to US fossil fuel subsidies. Their mission baldly states: "*The climate crisis is a reproductive crisis.*… As we consider having families, it becomes clear that the perils of climate change have made this a terrifying time to make such choices…. We now have to worry that the planet won't support our children." In related work also far from the infertility clinic, Katharine Dow studied ethical concerns about reproduction of rural people in Scotland building lives deeply influenced by and committed to environmentalism. She asked how ideas about nature and naturalness relate to views about parenting and building stable environments for future generations. Under such conditions, what is *today* considered "a good life"? What is "ethical?" How does this relate to "choice" about children for those who have such options?

An array of what we consider companion interventions to *Making Kin* has also begun to appear. For example, the Cambridge-based "Reproducing the Environment Project" brings together scholars working at intersections between reproduction and the environment both transnationally *and across species*, highlighting ethical and political concerns about the future, the quality of people's lives and inequalities between and within different countries *and species*. For example, one conference panel centered on "Reproducing the Environment: Climate Change, Gender, and Future Generations." Specific interests include how assisted reproductive technologies are used to prevent endangered species extinction (typically in zoos) and to improve food security (typically in university-based agricultural science), and how environmental conditions impact the ability to conceive *and care for* future generations (across species).

My last example of a generative intersection between environmental justice and reproduction concerns the current mass extinction of species of life on Earth, understood by scientists to be the sixth major contraction of biodiversity, and the first caused by (some) humans according to Kolbert. Extinctions have long been "incitements to discourse," generating toys, museum exhibits, movies, novels, and now YouTubes.

In *Imagining Extinction*, Ursula Heise analyses these popular culture discourses and related art-making. Her goals include improving public advocacy for endangered species *and* improving the supposedly neutral scientific tools involved in assessing ecological problems such as biodiversity databases and laws. Heise's findings allow her to elaborate new visions of environmental and reproductive justice accessible *across* species emerging today, akin to Haraway's "Chthulucene" as *transpecies* means of "staying with the trouble," and caring about and for a planet. Heise would agree that it is past time for extinctions to be incitements to feminist action.

Of course, many other such generative intersections exist, and our hope is that readers will be sharply attuned to finding them and making them known.

Toward Legitimating Making Kin

In writing *Making Kin*, we have rebraided threads of long-standing feminist concerns and activism about reproduction, environment, population control, and social and reproductive justice with new concerns manifest in the current situation, such as publically sanctioned expressions of white supremacy and fascism. As progressive feminists, we seek to remember our related pasts and hold on to what we have learned and gained at great cost. Through shared if fraught feminist endeavors, we have learned and are still learning how to speak of the silenced and the unspoken. We have learned to challenge non-egalitarian engagements that beset feminist goals albeit in changing ways, such as profound differences engendered by race, class, sexuality, nationality, etc. We have learned how to have conversations we have not known how to have when we started, conversations rife with difficult issues. And we have learned to foster institutional and other spaces and forums for new speakers, as yet unknown.

Yet today around the issues of making kin not population, and doing so with commitments to *multispecies* reproductive justice, a "booming silence" *including among feminists* has become part of the problem. If we don't speak out, attempt to intervene and provoke moving forward with alternative agendas somehow, some way, we are complicitous. So we have impelled ourselves forward. Here we go again. Or, here we hope to join other conversations and interventions we don't yet know of about these urgent issues that are surely happening elsewhere too.

We need new vocabularies for alternative futurities. We need legitimating vocabularies for not having biological children—both "childless" and "childfree" are already inflected/infected. We need an *elaborated vocabulary* for making kin and caring far beyond "pro- and anti- and non-natalist," and that does *not* use the binary-implying word "choice." UNICEF's latest estimate is that there are *2.7 million* infants and children living in orphanages around the world. We need further legitimation of and state support for caring for the children one has as well as for adoption and foster-parenting to provide children with safer and better childhoods, somehow *without* sustaining the horrific racist histories of stolen children and families. These histories are not only begat through colonial practices but also through carceral societies, failed wars on drugs, and failures of the state to support its citizens fairly and justly.

Further, we need these futurities to also legitimate having children and seriously supporting their flourishing among groups historically subjected to genocide, "ethnic cleansing," and the devastations wrought by colonization, plantations, and reservations—"stolen generations," "the disappeared." Replenishing stolen generations is absolutely vital for genuine reproductive *justice*. We also urgently need immigration policies across the planet to bring families, friends, and other life-sustaining collectivities together—major means of making kin in non-natalist ways.

Moreover, Michelle Murphy believes the word "population" has itself become so tainted by the racist politics of its historical usage that it must be abandoned. Here she offers the potent concept of "alterlife" for thinking through new ways of being and envisioning futures of distributed reproductive politics without it. Donna Haraway agrees that "population" is polluted, but believes it remains necessary to allow conversations and development of shared understandings *across* multiple and varied worlds, including feminist worlds, about problems of human numbers. Also, many robust scientific worlds are organized *through* use of that concept. "Population" is thus a problematic "boundary object" dwelling at the intersections of very different social worlds—highly charged, carrying multiple and even conflicting meanings, *always* needing to be deciphered.

The concept of "community" is barely more adequate. We desperately need better ways to describe how people collectively make and live more satisfying lives, especially as our "communities of commitment" are increasingly geographically distributed, making certain forms of caring more challenging. Older major relations have been denoted by informal "aunties" and "uncles" as well as "godmothers" and "godfathers." New(er) concepts for "making kin" still tend to favor familial metaphors, ranging from "chosen families" and "logical (rather than *bio*logical) families," to "academic daughters and sons," etc. But too many permutations exist today that go nameless, such as the male partner of a sperm donor to a lesbian couple who has for decades actively fathered the child, if not biologically. *Nameless relations can too easily go unlegitimated, hence are vulnerable to marginalization.* They somehow don't really "count"—even when they may be the most important of all. Many new concepts are sorely needed and hopefully are in formation, especially generated through more geographically distributed feminist collaborations.

We use the term "making kin" in two ways here—both processual. One is "making for the first time" as in reproduction or creating a new relationship.

But "making" also refers to the daily actions that transform partial relations into deeper ones, kinship crafted through the exchange of things, sharing activities, and other practices. This second sense of "making" is how kinship is sustained over time. Thinking about making kin this second way, we grasp that kinship can be blocked, broken, repaired—indeed the very ability to make, have and maintain kin can be stratified. People have varying capacities to make kin biologically, socially, culturally, financially, and perhaps most of all in terms of possibilities for being citizens together of the same country. Immigration, migration, seeking refuge each and all stratify the lives of those involved *and all their kith and kin* profoundly.

These and many related issues and committed engagements will inform the challenging futures of feminisms. Making kin and making babies and population are at stake differently, across people and species, across places, communities, and across different kin formations. This booklet offers some new (and old) beginnings. Yet we are anxious because of the urgent need to develop political analyses and ways of not only tolerating but nurturing and promoting difficult conversations and transforming them into actions. How can we as serious progressive feminists hold together despite what pulls us apart at many scales: absurdly unequally distributed suffering and well-being in reproduction and in making viable presents and futures for children and other species and ecologies? We seek to trigger something stronger than conversations while also recognizing how very hard and controversial kin making is and will be—especially non-biogenetic kin. We are well aware that our positions will require us to respond on different difficult fronts simultaneously. But we know too that we are building on strong foundations and have renewed passion for engaging and acting in these fraught times.

Overview of *Making Kin Not Population*

Making Kin Not Population is very much a collaborative rather than collective effort. As progressive feminists, there is much about which we agree, especially that population control strategies and policies are by definition anti-woman hence anti-feminist, and that reproductive justice, environmental degradation and climate change are urgent *feminist* issues. But our chapters feature different concerns, are often differently inflected about shared concerns, and also demonstrate some frictions. This introduction cannot do justice to the diversities of our positions. The authors' synopses of the essays that comprise the rest of this pamphlet offered next provide some orientation to what they view as our hopeful openings.

Ruha Benjamin (Princeton University) "*Black AfterLives Matter*": This chapter examines the relationship between race, reproduction, kinship, and feminist imaginaries. At a time when the everyday, extrajudicial killing of Black Americans is receiving global attention, the question remains: How do we make the matter of black life central to ongoing feminist agendas? Yes, subordination, subjugation, *subaltern*, literally "under the earth," racialized populations are buried people. But there is a lot happening underground. Not only coffins, but seeds, roots and rhizomes. And maybe even tunnels and other lines of flight to new worlds, where alternative forms of kinship have room to grow and nourish new life forms. Nurturing black afterlives is about enacting forms of kinship that encompass and exceed biological relatedness, from foster parenting and adoption to calling upon ancestors to fortify the living. Black people, whose reproduction has been *both* a resource *and* threat to the social order, have had to fashion elastic bonds of kinship to survive. The insistence on Black afterlives, then, is a commitment to cultivate kinfulness as part of the ongoing pursuit of reproductive justice.

Donna Haraway (UC, Santa Cruz) "*Making Kin in the Chthulucene: Reproducing Multispecies Justice*": Two immense and growing "populations" inhabit this paper: the Born and the Disappeared. *The Born* ones include the almost unimaginable (but countable in globalizing modeling operations) multi-billions of human beings, industrial food animals, and companion pets enterprised up to mega consumer status. *The Disappeared* include human resisters to criminal nation states, the imprisoned, missing generations of the Indigenous and other oppressed people and peoples, unruly women, trafficked child and adult sexual and other workers, Black and Brown young people, migrants and refugees, human beings subject to ethnic cleansing and genocide, and already about 50% of all vertebrate wildlife that were living on earth's lands and oceans less than 50 years ago, plus 76% of fresh water species. Both populations are crafted as global mass numbers by practices familiar to feminist critics of the state-race-sex-resource-and-capital making apparatuses of counting and inventorying. But both "abstract" sets of numbers are viscerally potent to me; they live painfully in my entrails and make me revisit the haunting practices of demography in order to propose, in the speculative feminist mode, a politics of making kin to craft response-ability for the conjoined twins that are the Born and the Disappeared. Her time frame begins in 1950 when the famous exponential J curves of population bomb fame show inflection points in category after category: human numbers, depletion of grasslands and soils, carbon emissions, mining extractions, displacements of people and other critters from homelands, the rise of mega cities, and on and on. Her question: how to imagine and practice multispecies kin making and reproductive justice in acts of SF (speculative fabulation, scientific fact, speculative feminism)?

Michelle Murphy (University of Toronto) "*Against Population, Towards Alterlife*": After decades of population control and the economization of life, population as a concept is too imbricated in racial violence to recuperate. To be against population is not merely conceptual, it is to be for the dismantling of the ongoing racist infrastructures aimed at materially sorting lives worth living from lives open to abandonment, injury, and disappearance. What other concepts, requiring different infrastructures and relations, might we come up with to bring together reproductive justice, kin-making and the struggle for more livable worlds? How to call out the distributed violence of choice politics for the rich, existing in worlds of white enablement dependent on pollution and dispossession for everyone else? This paper offers the concept of *alterlife* as a way to name the politics of distributed reproduction, and a project of non-innocently creating life differently together in conditions of ongoing massive violence. Creating alterlife on the Great Lakes draws together Indigenous Land/Body resurgence, the dismantling of settler colonial white supremacy, technoscientific potential, and the tracing of more-than-body relations, kinships, and responsibilities in the ongoing aftermaths of violence. Alterlife orients towards the many elsewhere-within-here of the past, present, and futures.

Yu-ling Huang (National Cheng-Kung University, Taiwan) and **Chia-Ling Wu** (National Taiwan University) "*New Feminist Biopolitics in Ultra-low-fertility East Asia*": After decades of varied interventions to limit populations and family size, East Asia now has the lowest fertility rate in the world, recently engendering an array of pronatalist policies. This paper analyzes three facets of feminist biopolitics through which to ponder and act upon such policies. First, it is urgently necessary to reevaluate drastic demographic changes by creating a new demography with new pro-woman conceptual tools. This must include replacement of the dependence ratio with new measuring tools, and the inclusion of women workers in projections of the future labor force (not currently done). Second, given threats to abortion rights and new risks associated with assisted reproductive technologies, seizing the means of reproduction has become a challenging and multi-faceted feminist agenda. Third, it is essential both to reorganize social ties of commitment to create social lives beyond traditional family bonds, *and* to strengthen understandings and ties across East Asia to engender more deeply *en*-connected societies, as we will explain.

Kim TallBear (University of Alberta, Canada) "*Making Love and Relations Beyond Settler Sex and Family*": This chapter interrogates settler sexuality and family constructs that have made both land and humans—

women, children, and lovers, for example—into property. Yet it is Indigenous families that are often characterized as dysfunctional. Indigenous peoples have been disciplined by the US and other nation-states according to a monogamist, heteronormative, marriage-focused, nuclear family ideal, which has been central to the colonial project. Settler sexualities and their unsustainable kin forms not only harm humans, but harm the planet. Here TallBear considers how expansive Indigenous kin relations, including with nonhumans, can be more relationally just.

****

As progressive feminists at this historical moment, we find ourselves again confronted with concerns about losing what we have already achieved, and fears of losing even more. We find ourselves in contradictory and at times even paralyzing positions vis-à-vis the issues raised here: profound concerns about the numbers of humans on the planet and the environmental consequences; the ongoingness of population control and the relentless demeaning of the reproduction of the poor; the continued lack of concern about contraceptive safety especially of LARCs; the decreasing accessibility not only of abortion but also of reproductive health care and even contraception; and on and on.

Regardless, we must reconfigure progressive feminist positions on demography and reproduction to fully integrate urgent environmental, conservation, and nonhuman species concerns. We know too that even with our varied voices raised, all the key points have not been made here. We sincerely hope that our work will provoke sorely needed fresh thinking, strong agendas and doable projects to facilitate making kin in new ways despite such profound opposition that in the US our current situation is called "the war against women." The challenges are transnational, but so too are feminisms.

1

Black AfterLives Matter: Cultivating Kinfulness as Reproductive Justice

Ruha Benjamin

afterlife \ˈaf-tər-ˌlīf \
; an existence after death
; a later period in one's life
; a period of continued or renewed use and existence
  beyond what is normal, primary, or expected

Vampirically, white vitality feeds on black demise—from the extraction of (re)productive slave labor to build the nation's wealth to the ongoing erection of prison complexes to resuscitate rural economies—in these ways and many more, white life and black death are inextricable. Racist structures not only produce, but *reproduce* whiteness, by resuscitating the myth of white innocence that inheres in the racial status quo. Racist systems are thereby reproductive systems.

In the US, our institutions are especially adept at resurrecting white lives that snuff out black ones. Exhibit A: On October 25, 2017, an Oklahoma judge ruled that officer Betty Jo Shelby would have her record wiped clean after being acquitted of murdering an unarmed black motorist, Terence Crutcher, 40-year-old African American father stranded on the side of a highway. *Wiped clean.* So as to remove any trace she was at the scene of a crime. *Wiped clean*, as one might do in a lab to avoid contamination, or a clinic to avoid infection. Reproducing white lives requires ongoing sterilization. *Wiped clean*, too, as with a baptism. White people are not just born once, but over and over, resurrected through law and custom, in order that they may kill with impunity.

If biological reproduction begets life, then social reproduction begets afterlives. White afterlife is, to be sure, a threat to black life. "Afterlife," in this sense, is a world of second chances. Exhibit B: In December 2014, the hashtag #CrimingWhileWhite went viral with white people across the US admitting to crimes for which they were routinely excused [quoted below as they appeared in original posts]:

> In college I punched a cop in the face while drunk but he drove me and my friends home.
>
> At 13 I stole a car with my friends & drove it 2wks before we got busted. Only one charged was black.
>
> #CrimingWhileWhite at 15, cops search a car I was in, found my weed, my switchblade + my vodka. they called my parents + gave it all back.
>
> Just got pulled over for almost hitting someone. Didn't have my license or insurance. Not even the threat of a ticket #CrimingWhileWhite
>
> I shoplifted when I was 14 and they let me go because my parents came down and we "looked like a nice family."

> #CrimingWhileWhite A bunch of bankers took down
> the economy and never went to jail.

To be white is to colonize the afterlife. Second chances
are the currency of white supremacy, "benefit of the
doubt" is the credit system, a "fresh start" is the return
on investment. If there is a Race Card at play, as so
many believers in reverse-racism claim, white people
are born with the platinum version and its killer
rewards program, in hand. Meanwhile, in a parallel
social universe...

Blackness is being born under a mountain of
racial debt. As Saidiya Hartman writes, "Debt ensured
submission; it insinuated that servitude was not yet
over and that the travails of freedom were the price to
be paid by emancipation." Hence enslaved black
people were forced to "self-purchase" their own freedom, for they could not even claim a property right in
themselves. Is it any wonder that, as Hartmann
describes, the enslaved used "stealing away" to describe
not only the act of running away, but also in reference
to a wide range of everyday activities:

> Stealing away involved unlicensed movement,
> collective assembly, and an abrogation of the terms
> of subjection in acts as simple as sneaking off to
> laugh and talk with friends or making nocturnal
> visits to visit loved ones... These nighttime visits to
> lovers and family were a way of redressing the natal
> alienation or enforced "kinlessness" of the enslaved.

Moreover, Hartman aptly dubs the perverse "political
arithmetic" that continues to devalue black Americans
the "*afterlife* of slavery—skewed life chances, limited
access to health and education, premature death, incarceration and impoverishment," and perhaps most of all,

devalued reproduction. If, as I have suggested, whiteness provides countless opportunities for rebirth, the racialized counterpart is a cruel protraction of life, how a torturer (or torturous system) works slowly, methodically, and viciously to render a fate worse than death. For that reason, reproductive justice extends well beyond the body—so often the site of trauma and exploitation—to encompass the full range of life-affirming practices that implicate the body politic writ large.

Black life is expensive, for sure, but so is black death. Even today, the kin of those who are unjustly slain are left holding the bill. Exhibit C: Two months after a grand jury failed to indict the officer who fatally shot Tamir Rice, the 12-year-old who was found playing with a toy gun in a Cleveland park, the city billed the Rice family for the dead child's last ambulance ride.

Racial debt is not only a product of black death, but also its precursor. Well before Michael Brown was murdered in the streets of Ferguson, Missouri, that municipality began exacting a pernicious form of economic terrorism that continues to extract millions of dollars in fines and forfeitures from its predominantly black citizenry. In fact, a recent study by Sances and Young You of 9,000 US cities confirms that municipalities with a higher percentage of African American residents are more likely to use fines as the basis for city revenue. As one observer put it, "It's easy to see the drama of a fatal police shooting, but harder to understand the complexities of municipal finances that created many thousands of hostile encounters, one of which turned fatal." Black debt, in short, begets black death which begets black debt in a recursive chain.

Before 29-year-old Sandra Bland died in a Texas jail, she was charged a $5,000 bail, which she could not afford. According to a federal study there are over half a million people sitting in city and county jails who have not been convicted. In 2016 alone, there were over 800 documented fatalities among those in lockup because they could not post bail. This is a form of "premature death" that political geographer Ruth Wilson Gilmore defines as a key feature of racist state

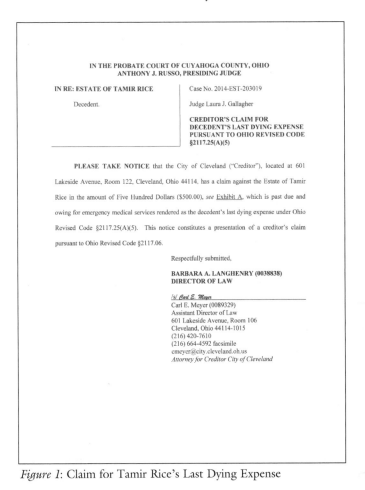

Figure 1: Claim for Tamir Rice's Last Dying Expense

violence. A perverse calculus of human worth presses down on kin and community, who are literally left holding the bill, financially as well as emotionally. Speaking at a Congressional Caucus on Black Women and Girls, Sandra Bland's mother, Geneva Reed-Veal, testified:

> What I'm going to say to you is that I'm here representing the mothers who are not heard. I am here representing the mothers who have lost children as we go on about our daily lives. When the cameras and lights are gone, our babies are dead. So I'm going to ask you here today to wake up. Wake up. By a show of hands, can any of you tell me the other six women who died in jail in July 2015 along with Sandra Bland? That is a problem. You all are among *the walking dead*, and I am so glad that I have come out from among you. I heard about Trayvon, I heard about all the shootings, and it did not bother me until it hit my daughter. I was *walking dead* just like you until Sandra Bland died in a jail cell in Texas.

In this testimony, we witness how waking up *after death* is a call for solidarity and an insistence that Black Afterlives Matter. It is part of a broader repertoire of invoking the slain to vivify collective action.

Scholar of modern slavery Zhaleh Boyd connects this form of invocation to the idea of "ancestral co-presence." She refers to hashtag signifiers, like #SayHerName, as gathering points that make present the slain and call upon recent ancestors—Tamir Rice, Sandra Bland, Michael Brown, Ayana Jones, and so many others—as spiritual kin who can animate social movements. Boyd further traces the relationship between this digitally mediated form of connectivity to the use of co-presence by legendary African figures such as Queen Nanny, Boukman, and Gullah Jack, who called upon ancestral powers in their fight against imperialist, white supremacist opponents. Co-presence, in short, troubles the line between the biological living and dead by calling forth spiritual practices of ancestral communication, now taking new forms via social media, yet retaining key features of African diasporic traditions.

Yes, subordination, subjugation, *subaltern*, literally "under the earth," racialized populations are buried people. But there is a lot happening underground. Not only coffins, but seeds, roots and rhizomes. And maybe even tunnels and other lines of flight to new worlds, where alternative forms of kinship have room to grow and to nourish other life forms and ways of living. In her discussion of more contemporary fictive kin networks in the African diaspora, Patricia Hill Collins explains,

> Enslaved Africans were property…and one way that many resisted the dehumanizing effects of slavery was by re-creating African notions of family as extended kin units…. Experiences of both being nurtured as children and being held responsible for siblings and fictive kin within kin networks can stimulate a more generalized ethic of caring and personal accountability…. At the same time, the erosion of such networks in the face of the changing institutional fabric of Black civil society points to the need either to refashion these networks or develop some other way of supporting Black children. For far too many African-American children, assuming that a grandmother or "fictive kin" will care for them is no longer a reality.

In the broadest sense, what is at stake in the idea that Black Afterlives Matter is the practice of making kin, not only *beyond* biological relatives, but also *with* the materially dead/spiritually alive ancestors in our midst.

Black afterlives are animated by a stubborn refusal to forget and to *be forgotten*. Hartmann explains that one of the main gatherings for which the enslaved would "steal away" was the praise meeting where the evocation of the ancestors was central to imagining freedom. Here they would enact "ancestral landscapes." In "remembering things they have not witnessed or experienced 'like when they lived in Africa and done what they wanted,' an insurgent nostalgia that expressed a longing for home that most could only vaguely recall or that lived only in the imagination transformed the space of captivity into one inhabited by the revenants of a disremembered past."

Figure 2: Paulleatha V. White, director of the South Central office of the Los Angeles County Department of Adoptions, and the author's grandmother. Ruha Benjamin, personal collection.

Materializing meta-kinship that exceeds biological relatedness continues to take many forms. It manifests in efforts to institutionalize kinfulness, in a literal sense, through foster parenting and adoption. My grandmother, for example, directed the Department of Adoptions in Compton, Los Angeles, the largest such agency in the nation at the time. She sought to dissolve the many bureaucratic and financial impediments that left so many black children stranded and kinless. Today this work is extended by organizations like the Children's Defense Fund (CDF). They developed a Kinship Care Resource Kit geared toward community and faith-based organizations to increase public understanding of the millions of households in which grandparents or extended family members are raising children. Running against the penchant towards social abandonment, black people have always had to construct their own afterlives through alternative family formations in the midst of crisis.

Born of necessity, perhaps, the cultivation of extended kinfulness is also a source of black pride. In a comedic take on the racial contours of kinship, writer Damon Young asks the million-dollar question: "Do White People Have Cousins?" Here he considers the "spiritual and metaphysical" dimensions of family formation by questioning whether race has anything to do with one's reverence for "cousin culture." This is a culture that dissolves the distinctions between first, second and third cousins and routinely includes those who "don't share any blood" into the fold of cousin-hood. He adds that one plausible theory for the relative elasticity of black kinship and the "buffering" role of cousins is that groups navigating hostile social conditions "need all the family we can get." In the end, Young acknowledges that there are likely regional (and

I would add, class) differences that challenge any easy Black-White distinction. Moreover, whether people imagine themselves connected based on a shared genetic code or as targets of a brutal legal code, bonds of relation may *bind* us even as they promise to—and do—buttress us.

However, when kin are the source of hurt or harm, it may in fact be wise to sever ties. Kinship, in other words, can be deadening when the obligations it entails are abused in and beyond the family. In a particularly disquieting example, Anne Pollock explains how the governor of Mississippi commuted the dual life sentences of the Scott sisters on the condition that "Gladys Scott donated a kidney to her ailing sister." Kinship, in this case, was enrolled in the larger project of mass incarceration and even though it was activated in the process of "release," the extraordinary condition imposed by the state exposes the coercive potential of familial obligations.

Kinship with the dead has its own demands and effects. Caring for the dead, even when not blood relatives, is a site where meta-kinship materializes in unexpected ways. Black Virginians, for example, are working to revitalize the neglected cemeteries of those who are not necessarily their biological relatives, but to whom they feel an extended kin obligation. They clear away foliage that hides long-forgotten graveyards and call for public support to memorialize the enslaved who are buried there. They point to the fact that the state has, for generations, earmarked funds to private organizations that maintain Confederate cemeteries, a practice that made *The New York Times* in an article by Brian Palmer. White Affirmative Action, it seems, knows no earthly bounds. But if material abandonment in death mirrors social abandonment in life, then maybe attending to "the needy dead," in Toni Morrison's words in *Beloved*, can disrupt "the order and quietude of everyday life," enlivening the memory and machinations for freedom of those restless underground.

While STS scholars like Haraway, Latour, Chen and others have done well in theorizing the different forms of agency exercised by living nonhumans, with increasing attention to the possibility of forging multispecies justice, for example in work by Kirksey and Haraway, there has been far less attention to immaterial actants such as those inhabiting the ancestral landscapes described above, with Kim TallBear as an outstanding counter example. In conversation with Indigenous metaphysics, Black feminist STS approaches to race and epistemology, for example in work by Sylvia Wynter and also Alexander Weheliye, not only disrupt the human-machine distinction, but also reimagine and ultimately refashion forms of spiritual kinship in which Black Afterlives Matter. Kim TallBear explains that she doesn't feel the need to adopt more "secular" language in her analysis, as she feels "comfortable enfolding spirits or souls into the beingness of nonhumans." With TallBear, I encourage ethnographic attention to afterlives as a necessary part of deepening our knowledge more broadly, regarding kin making and reproduction specifically. Situating the idea of co-presence in a Black feminist approach to kinship draws attention to everyday spiritual technologies, which typically remain buried in secular theorizations of technoscience. Again, there is a lot that happens underground.

Life After Death

Imagining life after death, and what it might mean to craft kinship with the dead, requires experimenting with fiction. The novel *Kindred* by Octavia E. Butler gives voice to the possibility of black afterlives in an exchange between Dana, the modern protagonist and time-traveler, and Sarah, an enslaved woman. Here Sarah tries to warn Dana about the dangers of running away from the Maryland plantation on which they find themselves:

> She lowered her voice to a whisper. "You need to look at some of the niggers they catch and bring back," she said. "You need to see them—starving, 'bout naked, whipped, dragged, bit by dogs ... You need to see them."
> "I'd rather see the others."
> "What others?"
> "The ones who make it. The ones living in freedom now."
> "If any do."
> "They do."
> "Some say they do. It's like dying, though, and going to heaven. Nobody ever comes back to tell you about it."

No *body* ever comes back, perhaps, but spirits and ancestors might. And here is where our stories of *what is* and *what is possible* matter. They produce meaning and material with which to build (and destroy) what we call "the real world."

As I have argued elsewhere, one way of experimenting with alternatives to the racist status quo is by employing speculative methods. In this moment of social crisis, where even the most basic assertion that black lives matter is contested, we are drowning in "the facts" of inequality and injustice. Whether it is a new study on criminal justice disparities or another video of police brutality, demanding empirical evidence of systematic wrongdoing can have a perverse quality—as if subjugated people must petition again and again for admission into the category of "human," for which empathy is rationed and applications are routinely denied. Consider the following stories of afterlife.

Life After Nuclear Fallout

When I was fifteen years old, my family moved from Conway, South Carolina to Majuro, the capital of the Marshall Islands, so my parents could begin working with the Marshallese Department of Education. The Marshall Islands are best known for the fact that they were the site of US nuclear testing from 1946 to 1958, sixty-seven tests in all. By one calculation, if the combined explosive power were split evenly over that 12-year period, it would equal 1.6 Hiroshima-size explosions per day. Needless to say, this history of militarism and imperialism continues to wreak havoc on the health of the Marshallese: "burns that reached to the bone...cancers in the short and long term," and congenital disabilities that cause babies to die hours after birth." One report sums it up, "The Marshallese are convinced that there is sufficient evidence...of inter-generational harm caused by radiation fallout."

Now add to this the widespread displacement Marshallese people have experienced, first for the purposes of nuclear testing and now as a function of US military presence. When I had the chance to travel from Majuro to neighboring islands, I was struck by how crudely inequity was engineered: Kwajalein, a US army installation was a manufactured suburbia, occupied almost entirely by military personnel and their families, enjoying golf courses, Baskin Robbins, and a yacht club among other amenities. The neighboring island of Ebeye is where islanders forced off Kwajalein to make room for the army base now reside in a crowded shantytown commonly known as "the slum of the Pacific." Ebeye residents require a special pass to travel to Kwajalein for work, while others barely subsist on the small checks the US government dispenses.

Needless to say, people are suffering not only from the history of direct fallout of nuclear testing, but also because of the oppressive conditions of their present lives—evidenced most readily in the high rates of chronic and infectious diseases including a TB rate that's 23 times that of the US, and occasional outbreaks of cholera and dengue fever. In this way,

Figure 2: Marshall Islands Sand Cemetery. Source: Vlad Sokhin. Published with permission.

military technologies are reproductive technologies—diminishing the capacity of those who are its victims to thrive, propagate, and imagine much less create their own futures.

Witness, for example, Marshallese children burying themselves in a make-believe cemetery—a reminder of how their lives have been biologically engineered—not in a lab, but in contaminated environments. In many ways, the Marshall Islands are a metaphor for modernity, in which the health and well-being of some are predicated on the immiseration, even slow extermination, of others.

Life After Sterilization

As a student at Spelman College in the late 1990s, I worked on a thesis project focused on how racism, sexism, and capitalism get under people's skin and impact women's childbearing experiences. About midway through the research process, I interviewed a classmate who told me about how when she was seventeen years old, she delivered her baby via C-section. As she explained it, sometime during the process, the doctor turned to her mother and asked, matter-of-factly, "While I have her open, should I just go ahead and tie her up?" The doctor, in short, proposed sterilizing my classmate without her consent, but my classmate vehemently objected. This was a full 40 years after famed civil rights activist Fannie Lou Hamer told her own story about checking in to Sunflower City Hospital to have a tumor removed, and walking out with what she later called a "Mississippi Appendectomy." In her words, "an unwanted, unrequested and unwarranted hysterectomy [was] routinely given to poor and unsuspecting Black women," usually performed postpartum. It was during this research process, especially talking with my classmate when I started to understand that, depending on one's social status, reproductive capacity may be celebrated and encouraged *or* disparaged and repressed, a rationing of agency that has been critically assessed by feminist scholars and activists.

This is not the stuff of dusty archives, put to rest with the passage of a few laws. Eugenic sensibilities and practices are alive and well. In the last few years, the coercive sterilization of prisoners has garnered greater attention and outrage. As late as 2010, an investigative report of California prisons revealed this trend; and in 2017, Derek Hawkins of *The Washington Post* reported that a Tennessee judge granted shorter sentences for prisoners who agreed to be sterilized. These "negative" eugenic practices that repress the reproduction of some are tied to seemingly more liberal, market-based, "positive" eugenic practices that encourage those deemed valuable to reproduce and even *select* the traits of their offspring. Two sides of the same reproductive coin.

In his classic text *The Souls of Black Folks*, W.E.B. DuBois queried, "How does it feel to be a problem?" In the context of our current discussion here, we might better ask, "How does it feel to be a... *population?*" To be a racialized population, after all, is to be a stubborn *problem* and an insistent *people*. To be subordinated, however, also entails inhabiting subterranean spaces where it is possible to forge new forms of kinship. Living life so close to death requires honing spiritual technologies to access the afterlife, calling upon ancestors, #SayHerName #FannieLouHamer, to vivify the movement for black lives. But first, some time travel…

Life After Earth

In 200 years, overpopulation on Earth compels humanity to spread across the solar system, colonizing Mars and the Asteroid Belt, where several generations of humans have been born and raised as Martians and Belters, respectively. This fictional world is the premise of a book series adapted for television, called *The Expanse*. Unlike many speculative tales, the series presents a remarkably diverse cast that challenges contemporary racial and gender hierarchies, while also signaling how racial vision and division may be reconfigured in the future. Human descendants on Mars are a formidable threat, physically and militarily stronger than others in the solar system, intent on engineering their new home to be more habitable.

The Belters, in contrast, are presented as weaker. Not only do Earthers and Martians dominate them politically and economically, but Belters are also physically more vulnerable. Due to the grueling conditions of life in low gravity ("low g"), they have begun to experience physiological changes like elongated limbs, bigger heads, and longer spines that set them apart from Earthers and Martians. Their language, too, has evolved into a Belter patois, which includes hand signs that allow them to communicate because they have to spend so much time in space suits. Due to the oppressive conditions on the Belt, where inhabitants are required to extract and export resources for Mars and Earth, Belters can barely afford the air they breathe, much less adequate food and water. This is a world of manufactured scarcity and precarity, not unlike our own.

In the future, as in the past and present, environmental exposures and social hierarchies are embodied. After several generations of living under such conditions, economic and political domination literally get under the Belters' skin. Not only are their bodies adapting to low gravity, but attempts to remedy the effects, like providing bone density juice to children, further exacerbate health disparities when people cannot access the medicine they need. In this world, 'kinlessness' is a liability as when low quality serum is handed off to kids who are wards of the state—a future that echoes back into our present where black children are shuttled through the US foster system at a dispro-portionate rate, a process well documented in Dorothy Roberts' 2002 book, *Shattered Bonds: The Color of Child Welfare*.

Thus, in a vicious feedback loop that should sound eerily familiar, unjust conditions that produce racialized physical and cultural differences further set Belters apart. Earthers and Martians point to these distinctions as "natural," evidence of Belters' inherent inferiority—justifying the continued subjugation of those whose land and labor (but not whose lives) are valuable. The physical differences that distinguish the Belters are not so much figments of the imagination, but *materializations* of a dominating imagination. Systems of domination require powerful narratives to allow those who hoard resources to sleep at night. Rather than acknowledge how exploitation and ghettoization *produce* the weak physiology of Belters, those in power view such physical differences as proof that the subju-gated are not strong enough to govern themselves. Through interlocking logics of racism and ableism, biological differences become indicators that oppressive social orders simply reflect the natural order. As M'charek states, "The factness of facts depends on their ability to disconnect themselves from the practices that helped produce them."

One of the main protagonists, a Belter named Joe Miller, for example, hides the "spurs on the top of his spine" with a hat—hinting at the racialized shame that attaches to disability. As analysts, we must attend to the materiality of spurs protruding from the backs of the oppressed *without* losing site of their sociopolitical determinants and cultural meaning. Domination burrows under the skin, converting structural inequalities into biological differences and mystifying the former in the process, so that, as M'charek insists, "the challenge in studying race is to denaturalize without dematerializing it, and to simultaneously attend to materiality without fixing race." In *The Expanse*, racism is not simply a carryover from humanity's past, but is reproduced and reimagined as a new yet no less destructive afterlife.

Fictions, in this sense, are not falsehoods but refashionings through which analysts experiment with different scenarios, trajectories, and reversals, elaborating new values and testing different possibilities for creating more livable worlds. And the work of peopling anti-racist feminist worlds abounds! In addition to Butler's stories, all of which remake reproduction and kinship in different ways, many other contemporary black, Latinx, and indigenous writers continue in this speculative tradition, from collections such as *Dark Matter* in 2000 and 2004 and *Octavia's Brood* in 2015, to writers such as Tananarive Due, Jewelle Gomez, Nalo Hopkinson, Andrea Hairston, NK Jemison, Nnedi Okorafor, Nisi Shawl, and Joanne Barker, among many others. In Barker's "The Seeders," for example, a group of women plot to overthrow a militarized star ship headed to the red planet. In Barker's telling, conventional antagonisms between humans and aliens found in mainstream SF give way to worlds in which indigeneity and extraterrestriality are not at odds. The narrator's indigenous kin are "from the stars." And even more relevant for this discussion, throughout the journey the irreverent wisdom of ancestors is called forth in the tradition of "co-presence" to guide dissidents struggling to fashion a *life after* Earth. Indeed, speculative methods are a mode of envisioning afterlives, extending present configurations of power and difference into the future to see how they might materialize and morph into (and beyond) our wildest imaginations. Rewind, now, to the present...

Engineering Afterlives

Terraforming planets gives way to engineering genomes. "Afterlife" in this situation concerns traits deemed desirable, worthy of extending their genetic life into future generations. Designer Genes, Couture Cells, Must-have Mitochondria. The newfound capacity to synthesize human biology raises fundamental questions of reproductive value. How we think about such genetic engineering has implications for all other arenas of social life and public policy, whether housing, education, employment, or incarceration. In deciding which afterlives to engineer, we select and reinforce criteria for what kinds of people to invest in, and who may be disposed of.

As reproductive justice advocates and analysts like Dorothy Roberts and Charis Thompson have long argued, water, food, education, and healthcare are *all* tools of reproduction, as they impact our life chances in profound and profoundly unequal ways. This more elastic notion of technology should lead us to consider how engineering human genomes is always already entangled with the assembly of municipal water systems, which is also connected to the structuring of tax codes, which is linked to the construction of racially segregated neighborhoods, which are manufactured in direct relation to the US prison apparatus in what Loïc Wacquant describes as a "deadly symbiosis."

Engineering, in the more generic sense, means to work artfully to bring something about, and there is nothing intrinsically "good" about the outcomes of sociotechnical designs. In fact, as a species, we have proven very adept at engineering inequity. So the questions we must now ask are: Is it possible to channel our tool-making prowess to artfully engender more just and equitable futures? Can we decolonize our afterlives, and make black reproduction matter as part of ongoing futurist, feminist agendas? Ultimately, reproductive justice entails crafting and imagining the worlds we cannot live without just as we dismantle the ones we cannot live within, where crafting and dismantling have as much to do with imaginaries as they do social policies.

For those whose ancestors were enslaved, the assault on black kinship is ever-present and pernicious. This is not simply a *byproduct* but a central tenet of maintaining white social order. Moreover, such ongoing regimes of social control and containment have led to new forms of natal alienation; for example, Murphey and Cooper tell us that one in seven black children in the US has had a parent behind bars. For the targets of institutionalized kinlessness, reproductive justice requires working deliberately and creatively to engender institutions and environments that foster a *kinful* existence.

To that end, I concur with a growing body of work arguing that prison abolition is a central pillar of reproductive justice because one of the most violent threats against black families and communities is the carceral system. Building on these analyses, I suggest that a black feminist STS approach to prison abolition illuminates the many technological fixes peddled as futurist, even "family friendly," solutions to the carceral status quo. Leading this trend is the popularity of electronic monitoring (EM) technologies to address the unsustainable overcrowding of jails and prisons and the social consequences of mass incarceration that Molly Carney writes about. Proponents of e-monitoring argue that such devices not only cost less and promote public safety, but also allow those monitored to integrate into work and family life as they await trial or serve parole. In short, such fixes are offered up as technical *and* social innovations, helping to sustain the kinship ties of those monitored, when in fact they *extend* scrutiny to entire families and communities.

As people who have been subjected to surveillance and those who have researched the implications of mass monitorization argue, its depiction as an "alternative" to incarceration is based on a number of faulty assumptions, and it should more aptly be called "e-carceration," discussed by Malkia Cyril. In the first ever report to analyze the proliferation of electronic monitoring of youth in California, we learn that e-monitoring entails a combination of onerous and arbitrary rules that end up forcing youth back into custody because of "technical violations." Attractive fixes, it turns out, produce new grounds for subjugation. These purported solutions appropriate feminist concerns about the well-being of subjugated groups, even while threatening the ability of black families and communities to survive, much less flourish. In many ways, such newfangled regimes of surveillance colonize life *after* incarceration. Making Black Afterlives Matter as a reproductive justice priority requires not only abolishing prisons but also deactivating the many innovative e-offspring that are falsely presented as more humane.

In contrast, innovating kinship takes many forms and employs a variety of methods. For example, Mariame Kaba describes a "Holiday Family Reunification" event organized by prison abolitionists to give incarcerated women who are criminalized survivors of domestic violence and sexual abuse as an opportunity to "spend a day with their children and other family members." Innovating kinship also materializes in the work of organizations like Mothers Reclaiming Our Children (Mothers ROC), mobilizing around the "symbolic power of motherhood" as a political identity to challenge the institutionalized kinlessness that locks away their children of all ages. Mothers ROC actively transforms mothers' "reproductive labor as primary caregivers into activism; the activism expands into the greater project to reclaim all children, regardless of race, age, residence, or alleged crime." In its early days, Mothers ROC organized cooperative radical self-help strategy sessions in the community room of a public housing project. Members soon began to extend their reach and reclaim space and power in the context of hyper-segregation and isolation—organizing a gang truce so family and community members could safely navigate turfs and participate in a public funeral procession for a young man killed by police. In the weeks to follow, they organized rallies and protests, and later developed a sustained effort that gives family members support and tools to demand justice for their children who are eaten alive by a ravenous carceral system. Cultivating kinfulness for Mothers ROC involved developing an analysis of and commitment to fight anti-black racism, while also welcoming Latina and white mothers of prisoners into their ranks. According to political geographer Ruth Wilson Gilmore, activists who engage in "social mothering" in this way present us a "glimpse of utopia's work" by mobilizing *across* the many boundaries upon which oppressive carceral geographies depend:

> They come forward, in the first instance, because *they will not let their children go.* They stay forward, in the spaces created by intensified imprisonment of their loved ones, because they encounter many mothers and others in the same locations eager to join in the reclamation project.... In other words, techniques developed over generations, on behalf of Black children and families within terror-demarcated, racially defined enclaves, provide contemporary means to choreograph interracial political solidarity among all kinds of "mothers" losing their loved ones into the prison system...

This "choreography," in turn, does not only take shape in connection with the carceral state, but also among activists organizing around education, healthcare, work, and all the many life-affirming projects that are severed in oppressive regimes of social control. Solidarity across differences is not a pre-existing condition but an outgrowth generated in the day-to-day labor of building political movements. *Reorienting ourselves towards kinship not as a precursor but as an effect of social struggle denaturalizes what kinfulness means and how to enact it.*

All kinship, in the end, is imaginary. Not faux, false, or inferior, but, as Alondra Nelson shows us, a creative process of fashioning care and reciprocity. Is it any wonder that black people, whose meta-kinship threatens the biological myth of white supremacy, have had to innovate bonds that can withstand the many forms of bondage that attempt to suffocate black life? Cultivating kinfulness is cultivating life.

2
Making Kin in the Chthulucene: Reproducing Multispecies Justice

Donna Haraway

Making kin in multi-modal, multi-species, multi-situated practices has never been more urgent. I call these times, our times, the Chthulucene to emphasize the ongoing powers and processes of mortal beings that come together to resist the curses and blandishments of the Plantationocene, Anthropocene, and Capitalocene. Making kin requires resisting both the category trouble and the practices of making population. That category and those practices are riveted to value conceived as limitless economic growth and are not committed to value as human and nonhuman naturalcultural flourishing through generations of earthly kith and kin. Those names, those commitments to value as endless growth, designate the end-making times of appropriation, exploitation, extractivism, and extinctionism for human and nonhuman beings.

In contrast, my prefix "chthulu-" marks chthonic lines and webs, materialities and temporalities of the earth, with no guarantees, no pre-set directions, no human exceptionalism, and no escaping consequences. The Chthulucene is full of the opportunistic sym-poietic liveliness of our mortal planet. *Sympoiesis* is about making-with, becoming-with, rather than self-making through appropriation of everything as resource. The suffix "-cene" (Greek, kainos, recent, present) marks presence in many modalities, times at stake, times for cultivating needed *response-abilities*, capacities to respond. The Chthulucene is the time to lust for multispecies environmental and reproductive justice, for still possible flourishing, for SF—speculative fabulation, science fact, science fiction—in the mode of speculative feminism. The term "reproductive justice," joining reproductive rights and social justice, was the potent contribution of Women of African Descent for Reproductive Justice in 1994. As Jenny Reardon emphasizes, "justice" is a "gathering concern" tied to stories for reimagining and redefining what is possible. "People come together to make another world possible in the presence of great trouble and enormous difficulties." Call that justice.

The Chthulucene needs slogans to rally its human and nonhuman peoples. Still shouting "Cyborgs for Earthly Survival," I propose "Make Kin Not Babies!" This slogan is a dangerous and partial, but necessary, sibling of "Making Kin Not Population."

I. The Born and the Disappeared

This is a brazenly personal paper and a plea for other-than-biogenetic kindred. I begin with a painful mass in my gut, pressing up against my diaphragm until it ruptures. The pain is much like the bodily feeling of grief when my mother died, when my first husband died, when my father died, when the dog of my heart died—the feeling of grief, exploding from the inside out, evisceration, terror. But the death of loved ones, and of one's own being, is the earthly composting of mortal ones, not a violation of some weird monotheist-inspired right to transcendence and immortality. Pain at such losses is intrinsic to living and dying well with each other as entangled tentacular critters of a rich earth.

But the pain I feel in my belly has to do with something else, something Deborah Bird Rose in 2006 called "double death," the surplus killing of ongoing-ness, the wanton surplus extinction of kinds, of whole patterns of living and dying on earth, of genocides across human and other than human groups. Double death produces what I will call "the Disappeared."

Coupled to double death, the pain slicing up my entrails has also to do with what I name "double birth." Double birth is the perversion of birthing (or hatching or germinating) of humans and of other critters such as industrial food animals into the relentless resourcing of all things terran into fodder for larding human numbers as a byproduct of extractionist, exterminationist colonialism and capitalism. This is humanism in capitalist modernity with a vengeance. Double birth is a parody of the grace of making and nurturing new ones of any species. Double birth—forced life for economist value production—produces what I call "the Born Ones." Child of post-World War II US white middle-class consuming affluence, I am one of the Born Ones. That is my speculum for this essay.

Thus, two immense, growing, and partially intersecting populations inhabit this essay: the Born and the Disappeared. Both populations are crafted as global mass numbers by practices familiar to feminist critics of the state-race-sex-resource-colony-and-capital-making apparatuses of counting and inventorying. Their reality is a specific, situated kind of modeled abstraction that works at a crafted scale called global. This crafting makes reality for everyone, but not equally, symmetrically, or exclusively. Other realities persist, in Indigenous worlds certainly, and also elsewhere in the belly of the monster where the lies of capitalist modernity make us blind, as Philippe Pignarre and Isabelle Stengers made clear. Still, knowing how the global is made does not mean it is made up, not materially-semiotically real. Abstract sets of numbers for the Born and the Disappeared are viscerally potent. They live in my flesh, and they make me revisit the haunting practices of counting and modeling in order to propose, in the speculative feminist mode, a politics of making kin—of making especially oddkin, off-category kin both inherited and cobbled together anew—to craft responseability for the conjoined twins, the Born and the Disappeared.

My time frame begins right after World War II, when the famous exponential J curves of population bomb fame show inflection points (steep changes in the rate of change) in category after category: human numbers; depletion of grasslands, forests, and soils; intensified mono-cropping; carbon emissions; mining extractions; displacements of people and other critters from homelands; intensified removals of human and nonhuman beings in the way of profit; radioisotope emissions; the rise of mega cities on every continent; breeding of billions upon billions of chickens, pigs, and salmon; and on and on. These conventional growth curves reconfigure global visualizations of naturalsocial necessity and the narratives of coming end times. These narratives must be interrupted by storying in the Chthulucene. Their steep slope changes in the years after 1950 are what I call the inflection points for Will Steffen and his colleagues' Great Acceleration: Double Death and Double Birth.

I approach these immense intensifications and multiplications of living and dying, of forced life and forced death in unprecedented masses, with the help of Jason Moore's arguments in *Capitalism and the Web of Life*. A world-ecological approach to demography would insist on the irreducibly historical, situated processes of all naturecultures. For example, human population increases, dispossession of land and other resources from both human and nonhuman beings, displaced peoples, and multi-species extinctions are not linked accidentally in the post-War explosion of soil-and-water extractive, toxic, industrial petro-agriculture across the world.

In a related but non-Marxist scientific idiom, Eileen Crist and her colleagues show the intersectional dilemmas of human population, food production, and biodiversity protection. Food production is a major contributor to climate change and the extinction crisis, with, as usual, those humans and nonhumans benefitting most suffering the least dire impacts. The super-peopling of the earth with both humans and industrial and pathogenic nonhumans is a worlding practice premised on the commitment to endless growth and vastly unequal well being. Alternatively, World-Ecology, Moore's term, requires conjoined naturalsocial feminist historical analysis of a kind that has simply not been done in demography, with its reliance on the conventional separation of nature and history in Western natural and social sciences. The crucially important 2017 "World Scientists' Warning to Humanity: A Second Notice" mends the gap somewhat, but there is a long way to go. Such analysis must be done if we are serious about making kin for multispecies environmental and reproductive justice.

An essential thread must be tied into the pattern of exploding destructive expansions after World War II, one provided in classic feminist intersectional analysis by Paula Ebron and Anna Tsing in "Feminism and the Anthropocene." How did the US model for growth become both globalized and mandatory? What were and are its main motors? To answer these questions, Ebron and Tsing have brought a feminist version of Friedrich Engels' 1884 *The Origin of the Family, Private Property, and the State* into the post-Cold War era of the Great Accelerations. "Race and gender were not just add-ons or ornaments of US leadership in modernization. They *made* modernization as we know it." Who became normalized and cultivated and who wasted and expendable are brutally categorized and produced in US-led Cold War expansionist projects and policies.

> White nuclear families anchored imagined "safety" while communities of color were made available for sacrifice. This formation of race and gender influenced Cold War and post-Cold War exports of US development, undergirding a program for systematic environmental destruction for the second half of the twentieth century.

Call that the Great Acceleration. Its machine tools were and remain racially differentiated, human exceptionalist, heteronormative, biogenetic, compulsory family formation and reproduction. Middle-class white reproducing families: the American Dream. Expendable populations of color everywhere: The American nightmare, including Population Bombs. Making kin differently is at the heart of feminism.

The Born Ones include the almost unimaginable (but countable in deeply flawed data sets and globalizing modeling operations) multi-billions of human beings, industrial food animals, and companion pets enterprised-up to bloated consumer status. The Disappeared include human resisters to criminal nation states, the imprisoned, missing generations of the Indigenous and other oppressed people and peoples, unruly women, trafficked child and adult sexual and other workers, Black and Brown young people, disposable young people of every race or ethnicity, migrants, refugees and displaced people, stateless people, human beings subject to ethnic cleansing and genocide, and already about 50% of all vertebrate wildlife that were living on earth's lands and oceans less than 50 years ago, plus 76% of fresh water species. The United Nations Refugee Agency estimated that displaced people, refugees and stateless people totaled more that 65.6 million persons in 2017. Nowhere are these kinds of counting done for humans and nonhumans together.

My question is simple: how to imagine and practice multispecies kin making and multispecies reproductive justice in sustained times of excess human and industrial animal generation, still intensifying plantation-system mono-cropping, forced lives across species, surplus deaths, genocides, extinctions, and disappearances? How to undo double death and double birth in sustained practices of innovative kin making? How to give each other heart to continue to care with our whole bodysoulminds? Let me continue with stories told using the genre conventions of Big Numbers.

The Born Ones: Humans and their Animals

I was born in 1944 when the human population of the earth is said to have been 2.4 billion people. In mid-2017 the world population was reckoned to be 7.6 billion. Carole McCann in *Figuring the Population Bomb* shows how problematic census figures are, but in my view they still indicate inescapable matters. I am white and female in a rich country and have been lucky, and so I am instructed that I have a high statistical probability of dying at 87.8 years of age. Let's call that 88 and look at projected global human numbers for 2032, namely 8.5 billion people (United Nations statistics). That is an increase of 6+ billion human beings, with a statistical confidence score said to be 95% of coming to pass, across one woman's life span, a 3.5 times increase. Models put the earth's total human population in 2100 at 11+ billion persons *if* birth rates continue to drop, as they seem to be doing all over the earth. At the *current* growth rate of 1.12% per year globally, which is quite low by 20th-century standards, the human population would reach around 19 billion persons by 2100. These Big Numbers say nothing about structured inequality and vastly unequal wealth and consumption, but they are also not phantasms.

It doesn't help that I personally did not birth any new humans; another sort of globalizing number tells me that my practices of living, however aspirationally green, extracted more from the earth (including from other people) than about 20 "average" people in Guatemala over the same period. Citizens of Qatar (not including the unentitled 2.2 million foreign migrant workers resident in Qatar in 2017, whose consumption is quite another matter) more than doubled my US American impact per capita. Oil has a lot to answer for. My unit of measure is called a comparative carbon footprint, a widely cited globalizing category.

No wonder I only partly jokingly call for a sliding-scale approach to global reduction of human numbers. Every living person of reproductive age alive today gets one token. Any person in a rich sector or region setting out to birth a new human baby must collect (let's say) 10 reproductive tokens from other prospective bio-parents, who may not participate again in making a new baby biologically. Of course, that in no way inhibits kin making and parenting; quite the opposite. The need for innovative kin making in such a system would be over the top. Each prospective bio-parent of whatever gender in less rapacious regions or social classes might only need 2 or 3 credits to participate in making one new baby. Those numbers would still be below population-replacement levels. Some areas of the earth have human birth rates that are already close to that. Instead of calling that a low fertility crisis, such conditions should be affirmed and supported in myriad imaginative ways. Persons belonging to groups subjected to genocide might need credits to replace and nurture the missing generations. No one imposes or enforces this sliding scale; the idea and all sorts of culturally specific practices related to it spread by infection, persuasion, and the joy of oddkin making. However, there are two rules that crop up in almost every sliding-scale formation in my speculative fabulation: anyone who tries to buy or sell a reproductive credit is condemned to spend twenty years washing dirty diapers (synthetic diapers will have to go, alas), more for repeat offenses; and anyone who gives their reproductive token to help make a new baby is committed to take action throughout life to make the world more child friendly.

There are more Born Ones to bring into the Big Numbers saga, however briefly. First, without even considering the toll in animal (and human labor) suffering, the global population explosion of industrial food animals has an impact on the earth in the same league as the other great extractive and polluting enterprises of the Anthropocene, Plantationocene, and Capitalocene. There is nothing comparable to the United Nations reports on human numbers, and so it is not possible to do a precise parallel for all the kinds of critters trapped in this globe-making machine, but the basic story is clear from sources like Tony Weis's *Ecological Hoofprint*. The huge increase in capture (called "harvest"!) of fish and other ocean critters must appear in both the Great Acceleration category and among the Disappeared, figures gathered by Lester Brown. The human Born Ones and the Born Ones of other kinds are intimately linked in their reproductive and world-making apparatuses. Also recent analysis of sixty-five years' worth of data shows that war, in addition to its scything human beings down repeatedly, takes an immense toll of large mammals across Africa. "And in explaining declines in wildlife, nothing mattered more than war—not human population density, the presence of towns or cities, protected reserves, or droughts." War is also a great driver of petrocapitalism. Given the horrific linkages of fossil fuels and industrial animals and plants in petrocapitalism, it is no surprise that the crushing growth of global human numbers tracks the uses of fossil fuels very closely and has done so for a couple hundred years, even as the biggest fossil fuel gluttons tend to congratulate themselves for reducing human birth rates soonest. The hypocrisy of the wealthy is mesmerizing. Outsourcing consequences is an old, sordid story. But there is the inevitable return of the repressed.

Not to be forgotten, the Great Acceleration since the mid-20th century includes vast numbers of market-worthy pets with consuming aspirations. To no one's surprise, I will consider only dogs. Pet-oriented websites give me my figures. The top two nations on earth now in terms of pet dogs are the United States, with about 75.8 million, and Brazil, with 35.7 million. Despite murderous sweeps of dogs daring to be on the streets before fancy international events like the Olympics, China is not far behind, with 27.4 million pooches, including many millions of so-called purebred dogs. About half the dogs on earth are not owned as property, and most get on with their free-roaming, statistically brief (but tenacious and interesting) lives heavily dependent on human waste; but the numbers of pets who are of interest to the highly profitable sector of pet product suppliers is immense and growing worldwide.

The Disappeared: Humans and Other Critters

There are so many sloppily counted disappeared individuals and so many poorly counted kinds of the disappeared: drowned migrants; dead Iraqi civilians;
bombed families in Aleppo; generations of brown,
black, and native youth across the Americas (forgetting
entirely the bones of African slaves at the bottom of the
Atlantic Ocean from the centuries of the triangle
trade); the fetuses and babies of the poor of Brazil;
low-end sex workers; the offspring of women sterilized
against their knowledge and will; invisible workers in
so-called informal economies; murdered transgender
and queer people; never-conceived but yearned-for
babies of non-heteronormative kindred; the forever
unborn of the youth pushed out of airplanes or buried
in mass graves in right wing coups in Latin America;
the missing generations of the Jewish dead from the
Holocaust; the missing generations from the displaced
and the war-dead everywhere; and on the list goes.
Casper and Moore detailed *The Missing Bodies* in 2009.
These missing babies, children, and adults are a matter
of reproductive justice and freedom, whatever else
these haunting ghosts are.

Among the nonhumans, the Disappeared are as
fiercely absent and hauntingly demanding. The Sixth
Great Extinction is not a metaphor; it is an unrolling
disaster. It cannot be stopped anymore. Perhaps it can
be reduced. Still, the extinguished kinds will not return,
no matter the heroics of technoscientific resurrection
biology. Writing from the lives of the animals, in *Flight
Ways* Thom van Dooren makes palpable what living
within the processes of extinction is like. In 2014 based
on a World Wildlife Fund paper, Damien Carrington
wrote about nonhuman extinctions and the steep

decline of wildlife numbers that have been outsourced to the less wealthy areas of earth as foods (and flowers) become more and more globally traded commodities, with all the implications for population displacements and land use rearrangements for both human and nonhuman persons and kinds. But the onrushing pace of provoked extinctions of kinds and of multispecies patterns of cohabiting beings can be moderated, and both old and new patterns of living and dying well can be nurtured. As both Anna Tsing and Isabelle Stengers argue in different idioms, partial healing in the ruins and effective resistance to ongoing ruination are still possible for so many who must matter in the ongoing tentacular Chthulucene.

There is no way to discuss making kin, including no way to imagine or enact reproductive justice and freedom, especially multispecies reproductive justice, without discovering the missing relatives—those with whom relations must be acknowledged—with whom necessary and enduring ties of oddkin must be forged for and by anyone who cares for mortal terra. This is a multispecies fabric with a key human thread. Central to the slogan "Make Kin Not Babies" is that all the human babies must be precious, not just those of "value" to 21st-century eugenic nationalist states, powerful ethnic or cultural groups, or well off families across terra. Committing to the biologies, cultures, and politics of making sure born babies can grow into flourishing adults is central to reproductive freedom and justice. This is not about "my own body's babies." It is about the Born Ones and the Disappeared and practices of making multispecies kin.

Before leaving the Disappeared, I turn to a reworlding event of comparable magnitude to the execrable carbon emissions and related phenomena driving today's climate change and extinction avalanche, namely the post-1492 depopulations of the Americas by the practices of European colonization and conquest and the consequences for the metabolism of the planet discussed by Lewis and Maslin:

> The arrival of Europeans in the Caribbean in 1492, and subsequent annexing of the Americas, led to the largest human population replacement in the past 13,000 years, the first global trade networks linking Europe, China, Africa and the Americas, and the resultant mixing of previously separate biotas, known as the Colombian Exchange. One biological result of the exchange was the globalization of human food-stuffs. The New World crops maize/corn, potatoes and the tropical staple manioc/cassava were subsequently grown across Europe, Asia and Africa. Meanwhile, Old World crops such as sugarcane and wheat were planted in the New World. The cross-continental movement of dozens of other food species…and human commensals… contributed to a swift, ongoing, radical reorganization of life on Earth without geological precedent.

Such an innocent-seeming word, "planted." It is not incidental that many of these foodstuffs were critical to feeding slaves and other forms of displaced forced labor of the Plantationocene and Capitalocene. And then I remember the wheat planted along the Russian River on the California coast in the 19th century to feed the exterminating European and US whalers. And the mono-cropped irrigated pesticide-sprayed wheat reducing rivers' carrying capacity for salmon in the Pacific Northwest in 2017 that Heather Swanson discusses.

Estimates of numbers of human beings living in the Americas before 1492 range from 54 to 61 million people. By 1650, the numbers were about 6 million, the result of war, enslavement, forced relocations, destruction of entwined human and nonhuman beings' patterns of living and dying, famine, and disease. The result was the nearly total destruction of Indigenous farming and use of fire, so that forests and other carbon sinks regrew, sequestering so much carbon that the result was rapid global cooling. The evidence is in the carbon signatures in old ice examined by today's scientists, just as recent huge carbon emissions are written into the (melting) ice far from the sites of production. To mark the change of geological epoch by the earth's carbon metabolism and resultant climate change, the period of foundational inventions of the Plantation-ocene after 1492 is as crucial as the fossil-fuel burning and related technoscientific orgies of the last couple hundred years. The Plantationocene marks the beginning of unprecedented homogenization of the earth's biota, which accelerated again after World War II in what is called the Anthropocene, but this time in ways that drive up the immense numbers of the contemporary born and disappeared. If the post-World War II period should be called the Great Acceleration, the period after 1492 might be called the Great Simplification.

If there are obvious dangers in thinking in terms of Big Numbers of the Born Ones—no matter how carefully broken down into situated places and histories attentive to inequality and naturalcultural specificity—there are equally obvious dangers in terms of writing of the Disappeared. For Native America, the most important point is simply that Indigenous people and peoples have not disappeared, but are shapers of today's worlds for themselves and for everybody else. At the same time, the depredations against the conjoined peoples and territories of Indigenous America have intensified in stunning acts of destruction and extraction. Marisol de la Cadena writes that "extractivism is how human geological force makes itself present in Latin America." Native America has experienced more than one end of the world, more than one mass catastrophe that puts the laments of Anthropoceneans convinced of the uniqueness of their experience of coming end times into perspective. Consequently, it is impossible to imagine serious opposition to today's Plantationocene and Capitalocene without aligning with the struggles and reworlding formations led by Indigenous peoples, as well as by other collective resisters, such as the Black Mesa Water Coalition. Such alignments are crucial to making human and nonhuman kin to loosen the fetters on present and coming generations from the Big Numbers of the Great Accelerations of the Born and the Disappeared.

II. The Trouble with Counting:
Numbering and the Undead Life of Categories

Those I hold dear as "our people," on the feminist left or whatever name we can still use without apoplexy, may hear neo-imperialism, neo-liberalism, misogyny, and racism in the "Not Babies" part of "Make Kin Not Babies." Who can blame them? Who can blame us? In her argument in this volume "Against Population, Towards Alterlife," Michelle Murphy shows why and how the mass-making mass numbers and categories of Big Counting, especially population, are still "designating and managing surplus life for the sake of capital." I agree. As Troy Duster also argues, counting is a far from innocent matter, and scrutiny of the apparatus for making data sets is crucial. Vitally, Murphy fleshes out a more generative way of thinking.

My whole formation as an historian of biology and science studies scholar, not to mention feminist, shaped me to know how "population" works as a category that makes worlds in its reproductionist and productionist image, a tool-image that participates in resourcing everything. I remember vividly the particular day forty years ago when I first understood that the population biology equations of ecology were materially, technically, experientially tied to the practices of the Metropolitan Life Insurance Company. Life tables took on a different meaning as I examined the hatching, dispersion, recruitment, and death tables of coral-reef species assemblages and studied competition equations derived from the math of thermodynamics, things I learned in biology and history of science with Evelyn Hutchinson and Sharon Kingsland. *The sciences of wealth and the sciences of life have gestated in the same toxic tanks*. With many others, I asked how biological knowledge might be shaped in other-than-colonizing-patriarchal-racist-capitalist apparatuses and categories. In the so-called science wars of the 1990s, those quests led some (especially some male Marxist) colleagues to call us "anti-scientific." That was their problem; ours was a lust for SF, science fact and speculative fabulation all together.

Murphy gave me Alison Bashford's crucial book on the long and complex history of Malthusian discourse, *Global Population: History, Geopolitics, and Life on Earth*, as well as Diane Nelson's searing indictment centered in Guatemala, *Who Counts? The Mathematics of Death and Life after Genocide*. We need other forms of numbering and assembling, something other than populationist frenzies in either the apocalyptic or developmental mode yet again. Further, I hold fiercely that the best knowledge practices across contemporary fields, including biology and evolution, foreground relationalities and not individual or massed countables. So why am I so unregenerate about holding onto the category of population? Or perhaps, so unable to do without contradictory ways of thinking at the same time? It feels like the same dilemma I felt when I wrote the "Cyborg Manifesto." Knowing that "population," as well as "reproduction," are the operators of biopolitics does not make them go away. Made is not made up.

It matters that I could not talk to other biologists about sea hares or brittle stars and their associates and habitats without the idioms of population. More than forty years of working and playing to open up idioms, categories, and ways of thinking in the naturecultures of biology have committed me to transversal and entangled relations of idioms in friction but not final opposition, to the polyvocality of categories and practices in situated usages, to the boundary-object quality of categories like population among communities of thinkers and actors who all care intensely about multispecies reproductive justice and flourishing. I learned how such boundary objects work in reproductive politics and sciences from feminists Adele Clarke and Teresa Montini.

In addition, I cannot forget the work that population thinking and counting have done to open up understandings of the apparatuses of inequality and to make inescapable the question, what is to be done? There are many current examples, but I will cite three from the 1980s and '90s. These are the kinds of scholarship that shaped me and continue to do so in the rich compost pile of fermenting new work.

First, in 1982 the historian of biology William Coleman published *Death Is a Social Disease* to show how a French founder of the public health movement began counting the dead over time in Parisian *arrondissements*, showing that the urban poor in early 19th-century France died at much higher rates than the urban wealthy. *Differential excess mortality* became an enumerated public fact tied to exploitation, subject to policy, not to natural necessity. Doing politics without these discourses would be very difficult. The idioms and categories are not enough, and they are not innocent, but they remain crucial. I remember learning in the 1980s from John Hogness, the Founding President of the Institute of Medicine of the National Academy of Sciences, how the Reagan-era deliberate failure to appoint middle-level professionals to empty positions in the US public health apparatus made good statistics on differential rates in disease and mortality much harder and sometimes impossible to obtain, thereby blunting opposition to cuts in social spending. What is not known as a public fact does not exist for public contestation.

Second, in 1993 Nancy Scheper-Hughes published *Death without Weeping*, in which she took on the persona of a "clerk of the records" to go among the coffin makers of northeast Brazil to count the invisible dead babies of the rural poor who never entered the national birth and death statistics. The result was a study fundamental to feminist anti-racist and anti-capitalist reproductive scholarship and politics. Counting the populations of the invisible is an essential feminist tool. It could perhaps be done without the idiom of population, but I think that would make comparative justice claims harder.

Third, in the context of US struggles over reproductive freedom from the 1970s on, African American scholar Charlotte Rutherford intervened forcefully with the differential statistics of race- and class-biased reproductive lives and deaths. She included Puerto Rican and Native American women and many more. No unmarked universal category of (white) women was possible. Further, the power of her argument lay in all the categories she linked to reproductive freedom in addition to the statistics of access to prenatal care, abortion, and the like: housing, safe schools, access to infertility care, freedom from sterilization abuse, toxins in neighborhoods, safe work places, type of employment, and more. Rutherford's paper remains a model of population counting and feminist justice work in the idiom of statistics.

The numbers in these studies seem different from the figures of global billions of the Born Ones and the Disappeared—more modest, perhaps more situated. But are they? What does scale do to the questions around "Make Kin Not Babies" and "Making Kin Not

Population?" Crafting scale and patterns of distribution are always germane to shaping shareable fact-based realities, to realizing and derealizing some worlds and not others. Making good facts is fundamental work for non-cynical, science-friendly, skilled adults. This is as true of "small" as it is of "big." The "global" is a relentlessly complex crafted reality dependent on category making and scale making. Lives and deaths of humans and nonhumans are in the balance.

And so I come to a conviction that I have formed over the last few years that anti-racist feminist avoidance of thinking and acting in public about the pressing urgencies of human and nonhuman global populations is akin to the denial of anthropogenic climate change by some deeply believing US Christians. God would just not do that to His children; there must be another explanation. Beliefs and commitments are too deep to allow rethinking and refeeling. For our people to revisit what has been owned by the right and by development professionals as the "population explosion" can feel like going over to the enemy. *But kin must be reconfigured in the contact zones, not on the fantastic right or wrong sides of these immense, complicated matters.*

I have been screamed at after lectures by my feminist colleagues of many years, told that I can no longer call myself a feminist, or that I am just a white imperial feminist after all, for arguing in public that the weight of human numbers on a global scale, however broken down by analysis of structured inequalities, opposition to ongoing racist population control programs, and many other important things, is an outrage. But the weight of the Born Ones is an extinctionist, extractionist pressure for humans and nonhumans. It is not OK to assign this issue to conventional environmentalists or population professionals or anybody else. This is a feminist issue. I tried to write some of this into the Camille Stories in *Staying with the Trouble*.

Denial will not serve us. I know "population" is a state-making category, the sort of "abstraction" and "discourse" that remakes reality for everybody, but not for everybody's benefit. I also think that evidence of many kinds, epistemologically and affectively comparable to the varied evidence for rapid anthropogenic climate change, shows that 7–11+ billion human beings living under any naturalsocial system so far imagined or practiced make demands that cannot be borne without immense damage to human and nonhuman beings across the earth and to the earth itself.

How can progressive people deride those who reject anthropogenic climate change for their refusal to listen to scientists when we—the same people—call the models of population demography nothing but modernizing ideology? Both sciences are based on model systems, big numbers, and imperfect data sets. This is not a simple causal affair; ecojustice has no allowable one-variable approach to the cascading exterminations, immiserations, and extinctions on today's earth. But blaming Capitalism, Imperialism, Neoliberalism, Modernization, or some other "not us" for ongoing destruction webbed with human numbers will not work either. Actual babies, and not just populations, are at stake. These issues demand difficult, unrelenting work; but they also demand joy, play, and response-ability to engage with unexpected others. Here's to Oddkin—non-natalist and off-category!

But off whose categories? Oddkin? Odd for whom? My analogy of global population counting and global climate-change modeling—both of which depend on elaborated apparatuses of diverse instruments and skills—breaks down at the same telling point: the self-invisible universality of categories and operations in a world full of other actually existing worlds, complete with robust practices of counting and ways of shaping possible realities. This is NOT a relativist point; it is an onto-epistemological one obscured by generations of colonizing power. Breaking down mass numbers and models of climate or population sciences into their complexities, while important, is not the issue. *The issue is, which worlds world worlds?*

There are many ways to deepen this point, but I want to return briefly to the work of Indigenous people and peoples in the current planetary dilemmas. For example, consider that the Inuit of the circumpolar north are exceedingly aware of the recent changes to ice, fog, location of astronomical points of reference in changed refractory atmospheres, animal distributions, and much else, but find the notion of climate change to be at best foreign, especially when extant and richly articulated ways of thinking and acting around "sila" (breath/life of the airs and land, reduced to weather in most English lexicons) better gather the people (human and nonhuman) to address problems. Why are there not well-developed contact zones between "climate" and "sila"? Not ethnohistorical comparative anthropologies, but active decolonial onto-epistemological and political labor in the face of sharable urgencies in the areas of the world where the ice is melting fastest, with immense consequences for the whole earth—and where the international race to control huge fossil fuel deposits has not cooled? Inuit ways of knowing are crucial, as discussed by Kunuk and Mauro. Kristina Lyons suggests a similar argument for the category trouble between "selva" (forest) and "nature" in

Latin American environmental struggles. Or between "hózhó" (right living, right relations of humans and non humans) and "carrying capacity" and "sustainability" in struggles around numbers of grazing animals on Navajo land over the whole of US-Navajo colonial relations, up to today, a story powerfully told by Marsha Weisiger.

Those who have not disappeared, against all the colonizing odds, have a great deal to say about making kin, about tying "relations" into worlds. Zoe Todd makes this case powerfully. Kim TallBear's chapter in this volume takes us much further into kin-making histories and current practices that remain unintelligible (or worse) to most non-native North Americans. She is joined by a generation of feminist Indigenous scholars changing the conditions of knowing and acting for all of us. This labor is important for population and kin as well as for geological categories. Numbering and modeling remain at the heart of struggles over lands, waters, airs and human and nonhuman peoples. In my natal Anglo idiom, this is about feminist multispecies reproductive justice and freedom.

I must stay with the trouble of a heritage I cannot disavow if it is to be reworked: the roiling pain in my gut from ingesting the mass numbers of the Born and the Disappeared. I am not free of these globalizing numbers because I think they still do necessary dirty work. The "Make Kin" part of my slogan seems easier and ethically and politically on firmer ground than "Not Babies." Not true! "Make Kin" and "Not Babies" are both hard; they both demand everybody's best emotional, intellectual, artistic, ontological, and political creativity, individually and collectively, across ideological and regional differences and across the work of uncommoning self-invisible universals.

Uncommoning the supposed commons is critical to building decolonial worlds, a matter that Marisol de la Cadena makes clear.

III. A Proposal in the Speculative Feminist Mode: Make Kin Not Babies.

My core question is simple: *How to ensure that babies are rare, nurtured, and precious and that kin be abundant, surprising, enduring, and treasured?*

Feminists of our time have been leaders in unraveling the supposed natural necessity of ties between sex and gender, race and sex, race and nation, class and race, gender and morphology, sex and reproduction, and reproduction and composing persons. I am conscious of our debts in this especially to Melanesians, in alliance with Marilyn Strathern and her ethnographer kin. If there is to be multispecies ecojustice, which must embrace diverse human people and peoples, it is high time that feminists exercise leadership in imagination, theory, and action to unravel the ties of genealogy and kin, and kin and species.

We need to make kin sym-chthonically, sym-poetically. Whoever and whatever we are, we need to make-with—become-with, compose-with—mortal earthlings. We, diverse human people everywhere, must address intense, systemic urgencies; yet, so far, as Kim Stanley Robinson put it in his SF novel, *2312*, we are living in times of "The Dithering," a "state of indecisive agitation." The Dithering is already written into earth's mineralized layers. Sym-chthonic ones don't dither; they compose and decompose, both dangerous and promising practices. To say the least, human hegemony and exceptionalism are not sym-chthonic affairs. That is what the Chthulucene signifies.

Kin must mean something other/more than entities tied by ancestry or genealogy, including population, family, and species. Kin-making is making persons, not necessarily as individuals or as humans. Making kin and making kind (as category, relatives without ties by birth, lateral relatives, caring, kindness, lots of other echoes) stretch the imagination and can change the story. Strathern taught me that relatives in British English were originally "logical relations" and only became "family members" in the 17th century. Go outside English, and relationalities morph and multiply.

Strathern was the first anthropologist to teach me that persons are composed rather than reproduced in Melanesia. Persons and kin are *compositions*, and growth does not have the same players, patterns, or imperatives as it does in Western production and reproduction, which characterize modern, usually capitalist accumulation, including accumulation of people as wealth. But Strathern is in a thick web of anthropologists who show that composing human and other-than-human persons occurs with great naturalcultural diversity. For my inquiry into "Make Kin Not Babies," our peerless editor Matthew Engelke directed me to Jane Guyer and Samuel Eno Belinga's work on wealth in (human) persons in Equatorial Africa before European colonization. Wealth in people had been mostly thought about in pre-European-colonial Equatorial African studies in relation to demographic increase or increase in goods tied to people (or people as goods, including slaves). But Guyer and Eno Belinga argued that what archives could be pieced together indicated that wealth in knowledge was perhaps more fundamental historically in this region and had a vast array of forms and practices.

Composing persons—and composing peoples—by joining knowers and knowledges of all sorts, from sorcery to understanding times for planting, was the source of much wealth, or perhaps better, was wealth itself. Acquiring slaves and/or trade goods, traders, marriage partners, and/or babies were not the only, or perhaps often the main, routes to wealth. *Composition, not accumulation, is the key.* Biological reproduction, production, and accumulation need not rule kin making—have not ruled kin making—in many times and places throughout human history, including now and here.

I join Guyer and Eno Belinga's exploration of "Wealth in People as Wealth in Knowledge" to a paper by Ed Yong reporting on a study among the Agta, a group of modern hunter-gatherers in the Philippines, who value story tellers over all other kinds of people, no matter how useful and functional other sorts of persons might be in their society. "Wealth in People as Story Tellers" intrigues me as a metaphor and maybe as a model for thinking about making kin in many historical and contemporary contexts. Surely as we face the immense challenges of human numbers and densities in all their political, economic, ecological, and cultural diversity in the next decades, story telling will be among our most valuable practices for coming to imagine and to know what is to be done. Composing persons and peoples through story telling is rich kin making. The Storied Ones are powerful affines, not by marriage but by pattern-making transformation, of the Born and the Disappeared. I remember that, like relatives, affines were mathematical properties connoting situated connections long before they referred to human kin.

The recomposition of kin acknowledges that all earthlings are relatives with affines, and it is past time to practice better care of kinds-as-assemblages (not species one at a time). Like justice, kin is an assembling sort of word. Laterally, semiotically, and genealogically, all critters share a common flesh. Ancestors as well as contemporaries turn out to be a bumptious lot; kin are unfamiliar (outside what we thought was family or gens), uncanny, haunting, active.

Over a few hundred years from now, maybe the human people of this planet can again be many billions fewer, while all along the way being part of increasing well being for diverse human beings and other critters as means and not just ends, in situated and webbed places with complex histories, not in abstract masses in deracinated space. Right now, we do not have a non-biological pro-kin anti-racist decolonial feminist politics, or even an imagination about what such a thing might be. Maybe the coming decades can be the times of the stories of the Children of Compost instead of the Born and the Disappeared.

Some things are clear. We must find ways to celebrate and support personal, intimate decisions to make flourishing and generous lives, including innovating enduring kin, without making more babies—urgently and especially, but not only, in wealthy high-consumption and misery-exporting regions, nations, communities, families, and social classes. Low birth rates are a good thing and should have a special celebratory holiday, replete with workshops on how the work is coming to support worlds for a few generations with much smaller proportions of young people than human beings have ever before experienced. We need women-and-men-friendly means of contraception that people really want to use, not imposed by population control programs that tend to privilege means outside a person's control, especially women's control. We need to understand that earthlings will be living with well over 7 billion human beings for many decades, while the proportion of young human people declines.

These are unprecedented material realities for everybody. No one knows how these decades will unfold, but that they will be hard is inescapable. We need to forgive each other big mistakes and take risks of inventive practices, old and new. We need to encourage policies that engage scary demographic issues by proliferating other-than-natal kin—including non-racist immigration, environmental, and social support policies for new comers, "native-born," and Indigenous people alike. People like me, white people, need to understand that for the Indigenous of North America, "native born" has functioned as an exterminationist, settler-colonialist category, which still works that way even while justifying old and new ways to shut the door against non-white immigrants and refugees. Comprehensive reproductive-justice policies must include education, housing, land rights, health systems, gender innovations, sexual creativity, agriculture, architecture, pedagogies for learning to nurture other-than-human critters, technologies and social innovations to keep older people healthy and productive, etc. etc. We need to make kin by dealing with the fact that many "populations" in the US cannot now and have not been able for hundreds of years to bring up children in safety, much less abundance. As both Alondra Nelson on the panel titled Make Kin Not Babies at the meetings of the Society for Social Studies of Science in 2015 and Ruha Benjamin in this book make abundantly clear, Black Lives Matter is a feminist kin-making movement, among many other things.

Babies—there are plenty of babies among the born ones, just not the "right sort" for the resurgent nationalist and eugenicist and hetero- and homonormative family-oriented pronatalists. The born ones deserve real pro-baby, pro-child worlding, not state policies and technosciences only for the "right kind" of new babies. Refugee children and foster children—as well as resettled refugees and former foster youth who have aged out of public support systems—need ongoing kin-making community practices. There are many examples of people making a difference, but it is not enough. The born ones need each other and all the critters of terra. They deserve a world that has not been surveyed, numbered, mapped, and resourced for nothing but more humans in endless human exceptionalist projection and extraction, under whatever ideological screen.

The personal "right" (what a word for such a mindful bodily matter!) to birth or not to birth a new baby is not in question for me; coercion is wrong at every imaginable level in this matter, and it tends to backfire in any case. On the other hand, what if the new normal were to become a cultural expectation that every new child have several lifetime committed parents (who are not necessarily each other's lovers and who would birth no more new babies after that, although they might live in multi-child, multi-generational households)?

I am filled with cascades of questions.

What if serious lateral adoption practices for, of, and by the elderly and other adults and youth became common? How to expand adoption practices of savvy situated kinds in many places? What if nations that are worried about low ("native") birth rates and demographic change (Denmark, Germany, Japan, Russia, Taiwan, white America, more) acknowledged that fear of immigrants is a big problem, as well as fear of "minorities," and that racial purity projects and fantasies, not to mention ageism, drive resurgent pronatalism by the wealthy? Perhaps even Paul Ryan, Speaker of the US House of Representatives, could be brought to account for his anti-immigrant nationalist pronatalism in the middle-class, white-normative reproductive, nuclear family mode.

What if making a new baby became truly an act of joy and material, daily responsibility for an enlarged community? How to celebrate children in non-natalist movements? "Child care" does not begin to name what is needed and must become normal. What if people everywhere looked for non-natalist kin-making innovations to individuals and collectives in queer, decolonial, and Indigenous worlds, instead of to European, Euro-American, Chinese, or Indian rich and wealth-extracting sectors?

How to nurture, identify, and promote durable multi-generational non-biological kin-making, as well as support other forms of family, including conventional reproductive families, while earth humans transition to vastly less reproduction and vastly more imaginative kin-making, in diverse, situated worlds in and out of the US? How to recognize and empower the many ways diverse peoples do and have done person-making and kinship-making, without imperatives to increase human numbers or reduce the worlds of nonhumans? How to support women and others in non-natalist decisions and ways of flourishing across generations and in many cultures, religions, peoples, economies, regions, and nations? How to celebrate human maturity for women and men in building selves and communities without making babies? How to nurture new subjectivities for old and young about babies and children? How to be seriously pro-moms (and other sorts of parents) without needing new babies to do it? How to develop recognized, structurally supported sibling practices for non-biological siblings? How to nurture queer kin-making of known and unknown kinds?

How to counter pro-natalism by empowering actual babies in need of a truly pro-child world? How to energize the born ones who are committed to ending double death and double birth, both of which are killers of ongoingness? How to empower kin making in immigration as well as stable residence, and in efforts to reconstitute lives in the death zones of war and extraction? How to build nonbiological kin-making technologies and sciences (housing, social-support sciences and technologies, food systems, multispecies community sciences and technologies, medicine, and more)? How to encourage science-art collaborations for pro-kin, non-natalist practices and policies? How to tell new stories to sustain needed new worlds?

How to increase human and multispecies well being as means and not just ends, while radically reducing human demands and radically repairing damaged life worlds and places across the planet? How to reintroduce caring about earth at every scale, how to do this without reintroducing racist environmentalist or populationist discourses, practices, and fears? How to understand pro-kin, non-natalist thinking and action from the point of view and agency of peoples who have been and are now subject to genocide and violent population reduction through conquest, disease, poverty, and war? How to build solidarities with peoples who need more babies, even while most peoples and communities must learn to flourish with many fewer new babies? How to become smart and imaginative about and with human and nonhuman peoples? How to be simultaneously against population control apparatuses, like those reported by Kalpana Wilson, and for a less human-heavy world through parent-and-child friendly means? How to think and act while knowing the trouble with the category of population, with its abstract economized masses, while not dodging the hard, dangerous work of facing questions about making babies in human-heavy worlds? Making many fewer new babies in situated and power-sensitive reworldings is not the entire project of multi-species environmental and reproductive justice—far from it—but it is an inescapable thread in the weave.

How to become feminist again for the whole person, whole community, whole earth? Can the idiom of whole anything be spoken without imperializing universalist fantasies? Feminist science studies cannot be consumed by genetics, biological and technological reproduction, and related foci. Enough! Where are our utopian, risky imaginings and actions for earthlings on a mortal, damaged, human-dense world?

So, make kin not babies! Make kin not population! It matters how kin make kin.

Figure 1: Artwork by Elaine Gan. Published with permission.

3
Against Population, Towards Alterlife

Michelle Murphy

A group of individuals and the sum of inhabitants. Population is pervasively used as a neutral term that abstractly describes a multitude. Yet figures of massified life, in the forms of crowds and overpopulation, have been persistently racializing. With intensifying climate change, mass extinctions, and extraction regimes poisoning lands, airs and waters, the problem of overpopulation has been recharged for left and liberal politics as a way to think through environmental crisis. In media venues like *The Guardian*, aerial photos of global slums and crowded shopping malls excite privileged viewers to reattach anxiety to overpopulation.

This essay takes a position against population as a framework for a feminist politics while still elevating the question of reproductive politics in feminist decolonial environmental justice. Even if population as a framework is abandoned, it is also the case that an individualized approach to reproductive justice, in which the individual and their right to choice only takes precedence, is also an inadequate framework for addressing the mesh of responsibilities and entanglements reproduction has with environmental violence. Following in the footsteps of a multitude of radical reproductive justice visions, might we search for concepts that reframe reproductive justice as fundamentally a concern of environment—that is of land, water, non-human relations, hostile conditions, and life supports in worlds already damaged? This essay opens a critical path against population and moves towards a reparative path, envisioning a distributive reproductive politics that stretches beyond bodies, choice, and babies to extensively include all our relations and responsibilities within damaged worlds.

Achieving distributive reproductive justice requires creating infrastructures that disseminate viable worlds, queer and non-human kinships, harm reduction practices, and also the taking apart of violent systems. What concepts might be given up to make room for other ways of creating a politics of reproductive justice? Population is not the only way to think through a politics of more-than-individual reproduction that is responsible to environmental violence. Hence, I make my case beginning with a refusal of population and then move towards positing the beginning of something else: the concept of alterlife.

Against Population

While we can trace population thinking back to Malthus in the 18th century, the managerial sense of population—as a quantity problem fixed by *adjustable* birth and death rates—is a 20th-century formulation. Population, in the 20th century, became a calculative concept used to govern the stock of people in a nation-state for the sake of economic productivity. In 19th-century Britain, the term designated the working class as an undifferentiated mass, and in mid-20th-century United States, the word named the totality of people in a prison. Population, as an artifact of a particular way of counting, bundles up bodies into a single tally, creating distance and abstraction for a managerial gaze that is then poised to ask, "What should be done about *them*?" It is a formulation that allows the anonymization of lives into deletable data points.

The histories of the uses of "population" are ignored at our peril. I have tried to show this in *The Economization of Life*, building on works by Alison Bashford, Betsy Hartmann, Farida Akhter, and many other chroniclers of eugenics and population control. In the first half of the 20th century, the problem of population was politicized in nations around the world as the eugenic project of racial futures, how to prevent the breeding of some for the sake of the evolutionary future of the whole. The word "prevention" here hides the vast range of violences undertaken in the name of racial evolution: sterilization, segregation, child-theft, residential schools, incarceration, starvation, murder, war. The future of population was often posed as the problem of differential fertility, creating national projects of destructive sorting: the problem of poor people having more children than the rich, of blacks having more children than whites, of the colonized having more children than the colonizer. From Malthus to American foreign policy, the problem of population has been framed as a way to avert crises, as necessitating unsavory acts in order to thwart a potential apocalypse of starvation, resource depletion, and war.

In the cold war/postcolonial/ongoing-settler colonial period of the second half of the 20th century, when it became less allowable for scientific and political elites to explicitly invoke racial biological difference as a sufficient rationalization for violent policies, the problem of population was transformed within the social sciences into the dilemma of too many people: the problem of the prevention of the birth of surplus others for the sake of future economic prosperity of the nation. In the UN, USAID, and national population departments around the world, population became a concept affectively charged with a fear of future apocalypses caused by the too-many. Population became a kind of simple quantification of mass, containerized by the project of nation-statehood. It joined Gross National Project as a simple kind of measure, one meant for adjustment: population and economy *together* needed to be counted, stimulated, managed. Economy's perpetual growth required population's curbing. In the second half of the 20th century, every nation was required to offer up such numbers as the price of participation in transnational agreements and finance.

But so too was population summoned as a problem modeled as a planetary-scaled phenomenon open to ongoing management, legitimating projects incorporating American interests to cover the globe. Population, as worked through the now globalized practices of population control since the 1960s, has rested on calculations of surplus life and white supremacy, of foreign life to be kept outside of borders, of lives not worth saving, of killable brown and black others, and of elite lives to be protected. The concept of population has worked its way deep inside conventional policy, economic, ecological, and life science thinking. Trained to inhabit a world composed of objects and forces rendered by these epistemologies, critics of environmental violence, especially biologists, might find it difficult to imagine a future organized without "population" as a concept.

Yet the problem of population is not just conceptual. Population as a problem carries with it thick transnational webs of infrastructures, laws, experimental platforms, clinics, and technologies of population control still in operation today. Population infrastructures continue to weaponize birth control practices, distributing coercive sterilization, inventing new flexible forms of eugenics, propagating extractive experiments, putting up border walls, and fomenting racist violence. Population is bound to the material horror of genocide, apartheids, sexual violence and colonialisms. Each is animated by designations of life as expendable.

After spending over a decade in the thick archive of data produced by histories of the experimental exuberance of globalized family planning in American empire, after reading thousands of studies about averting the births of poor, Indigenous, brown, and black people, studies in which race is rarely mentioned even as it is the very grammar of designations of surplus life, after living with the ongoing violence of settler colonialism in Canada, population has become for me an intolerable concept. I am against population. #AgainstPopulation

Not only is population a way of managing human presence saturated with racism, concentrating fears on the problem of population is also a distraction. It deflects from the crucial fact that it is the structures of industrial accumulation, militarism, and consumption—justified by the goal of improving macroeconomic measures—that have overwhelmingly produced the material violence of climate change, extensive planetary pollution, and death-making terraforming. A 2017 Major Carbons Database report identifies just 90 companies that are responsible for two-thirds of the last 150 years of green house gas emissions. In this moment of intensifying environmental violence, human density is attractive as a managerial policy problem and container for worry because it points the finger at preventing future human life without requiring the reordering of capitalism, colonialism, the nation-state, or heteropatriarchy as world orders. If only there were fewer humans in sites of high-human density, then future others might live more abundantly. Population policies of every flavour imaginable have been tried over the last half century, and they have resoundingly failed to curb the violence of the world.

Instead, nearly a century of governing industry for the sake of growing the national macroeconomy has produced a globalized capitalist infrastructure that, on the one hand, produces the molecular material "waste" of emissions as outside of the calculation of value and, on the other hand, designates poor people as forms of human "waste," better for the world to be without, and hence correspondingly open to abuse, abandonment, and elimination. In other words, population as a concept is enmeshed in the very infrastructures and logics that have produced ubiquitous environmental violence.

The problem of massive, widely distributed, environmental violence has today reinstalled population as an affectively charged problem. Categories like climate change and the Anthropocene offer planetary-scaled renderings that calibrate well with the framework of population. Charts demonstrating the "Great Acceleration" put the dramatic upward slope of human population next to those of extinction, carbon dioxide, and pollution emissions. This earth systems optics of Anthropocene, as Joseph Masco has shown, is caught up in cold war American military histories of planetary-scaled measurement, planning, and nuclear war modelling. It is thus no accident that population thinking (with its own entanglements with cold war military global planning, and not just ecological modelling) fits well within the units of analysis of the Anthropocene. Narratives of the Anthropocene emphasize environmental violence at the totality of the planetary combined with an imminent apocalyptic horizon that, together, encourages responses crafted as massive and urgent, hence assembling the enormous earth system scale of problematizing with the ethically fraught timescape of the emergency as a justification for suspending ethics. For whom do these scalings of the problem make sense? Population is not the only way of thinking through reproductive politics in relation to intensive environmental violence, even if the inheritance of cold war and colonial epistemologies keep offering population as a container. Given the existence of elaborate national and transnational projects to reduce population in the 20th century, is there any surprise that it remains easier to imagine doing something about population than ending capitalism? I do not believe that a radical political imaginary for the concept of population can be mobilized without amplifying existing infrastructures already deployed towards racist necropolitical ends. To take a stance against population is to prompt the challenge of recognizing and creating other ways of figuring humanity, relations, and density as part of collectivities resisting environmental violence and towards more livable worlds.

So how to talk about intensive human-caused environmental violence and its relation to the questions of human presence, distributions of reproductive possibility, and differential exposures to death? How do reproductive politics and massive environmental violence connect? How to create a politics of reproduction beyond the myopia of the individual body and in recognition of macrological political dimensions of human life, and even all being? This essay is an attempt to think through these questions in, alongside, and in struggle with colleagues and mentors whose work, it is no exaggeration to say, have made my own possible. It is an attempt to think futures and concepts in the spaces between conflicting and yet deeply entangled feminisms. And it is an insistence of opposition to population and human numbering as a feminist framing for land defense while still puzzling through how reproductive politics is integral to environmental justice.

For some, particularly people in privileged vantage points, the abuses of population control are parried with a politics of individual choice and the individual right to choose to have or not have children. However, women of color, Indigenous, queer, and decolonial feminist reproductive justice has long been critical of this privileged version of reproductive politics, which pivots on the well-resourced individualized user and consumer of reproductive health care services and commodities. Reproductive justice frameworks built by organization such as the Sister Song Women of Color Reproductive Health Collective, Asian Communities for Reproductive Justice, or Native Youth Sexual Health Network emphasize building strategies of *community*, not just individual, survival and flourishing. Radical reproductive justice takes as its starting point the *affirmative making of the conditions that support collective life* in the face of persistent racist, colonial, and heteropatriarchal life-negating structures. Thus, reproductive justice bleeds into environmental justice, which includes water, land, and non-human relations, as well as policing, food, shelter, schools, reserves, carceral systems, war, structural unemployment, and pollution. If you cannot drink the water, there is no reproductive justice. Or, as the Third World Women's political banner at a 1979 Boston protest about murdered Black women declared, "We cannot live without our lives."

So if conditions of environmental hostility require versions of collective reproductive justice, might the same be said of elite and enabled life? What reproductive justice politics can grapple with rich, white, settler colonial, heteronormative reproduction, of baby-making with expensive strollers assembled in supply chain capitalist webs, of fossil-fuel guzzling SUVs fed through pipelines, of oil turned into piles of plastic toys destined for landfills and then microplastic gyres, of white property relations with empty rooms, of grocery stores stocked with the bright goods of multi-national corporations, and all the many forms of white possession and enablement? Reproduction here is not just the baby. Webs of relations and distributions of violence make possible the smooth life of abundant choice. This kind of reproductive accumulation is another kind of density—a density of relations that enable capitalist life at the expense of all else. Here we can think of density in a different way: not in terms of human numbers, but as densities of relations that create the enablement and entitlement that in turn depend on and propagate often quite distanced distributions of violence.

What responsibilities to webs of injury, land theft, and other worlds does an anti-colonial, anti-racist environmental reproductive justice politics attuned to the environmental violence of capitalism, white supremacy, and settler colonialism demand? What responsibilities to our entanglements in webs of accumulation, entitlement, and hoarding? An extended, anti-racist and decolonial reproductive justice politics stretches beyond babies, birth and bodies and out into struggles of survival that are not just personal survival, but struggles over what more-than-life relations might persist into the future for collectivities. It also asks what relations should be dismantled, refused, shunned? This extensive sense of reproductive relations thus includes policing and military violence, reserves and borders, heterosexuality and family, property and labor, land and water, and questions of redistribution of resources and life chances. It includes Black Lives Matter, Missing and Murdered Indigenous Women, Girls, and Two Spirit People, No One is Illegal, and countless struggles against extractive regimes around the globe.

A distributed reproductive politics is not about birth rates or human numbers. It is about which kinships, supports, structures, and beings get to have a future and which are destroyed. A distributed reproduction is not about babies in particular (neither is it against them); instead its ambit extends into air, water, land, and a mesh of life forms into the multigenerational future. It is not merely about how bodies reproduce, it is about how life supports are replenished, cared for, and created. It is inseparable from a becoming-with-the-many that includes shelter, technologies, protocols of governance, structures of violence, animals, plants, ancestors, and histories. A distributed sense of reproduction attends to what infrastructures, assemblies, systems, and collectivities are supported through violence—capitalism, colonialism, white supremacy, heteropatriarchy—and what relations must struggle for their continuity or resurgence, and in so doing fight for the destruction of those violent systems, a dismantling that makes room for other forms of life. As Winona LaDuke asserts, not pipelines for oil, but for water. Which structures have to end to make room for livable ways of being together? The list is long. Reproduction (as perpetuation) is not in itself an inherent good.

Aspiring towards decolonizing and queer alter-worlds, reproduction might be better rethought as a politics of redistributing relations, possibilities and futures. #RedistributionsNotReproductions. Making redistributed relations is an extensive, ongoing endeavor, looped with imperfections, messiness, returns and futurities. I am against population and for a politics of differently distributed futures. #DifferentFutures

So to be against population is to reject the zeroing in on human density and wealth as problems of disconnected counting and to instead concentrate political attention on decomposing the density of consumption, property, waste and state sanctioned violence that prop up capitalism, colonialism, and white supremacy, while at the same time creating less violent ways of being with land. It is to struggle over different futurities, not differential fertility. To be against the problem of population, then, calls for concepts and practices of becoming-with-the-many-differently that resist the impulse of the biopolitical equation: "some must die so that others might live." It is not to be against numbers or science in total, but rather particular ways of doing numbers. To be against population is also to reject the proprietary heterosexual family form that the storm of capitalism, racism, colonialism, and liberalism demands as the container for reproductive choice. To be against population is to foster a multitude of ways of living in kinship differently that already exist all around us, as well as to continue to create speculative otherwises.

Towards Alterlife

At stake in conjuring alter-collectivities and redistributions is the very sense of what constitutes life, land, and its relations. Refusing population as a unit of analysis opens up an invitation to transform the many obsolete and violent epistemic habits sedimented into scientific ways of problematizing life. Within the biological sciences, there is no unified theory of life, even as the units of gene, body, species, and ecosystem have become so commonplace that they seem to exist in the world itself, and not as historically particular materializations of it. Making futurities in the aftermaths of ongoing violence requires alternative decolonial ways of retheorizing life with and against, alongside and athwart, technoscientific framings of life and environment. It is to learn from and propagate politics and concepts in the tensions between violences that have already happened and the need to undo them nonetheless, the condition of being already altered and the struggle to become otherwise in the aftermath.

In this spirit, I share from an experiment in learning with the concept of *alterlife*—the struggle to exist again *but differently* when already in conflicted, damaging, and deadly conditions, a state of already having been altered, of already being in the aftermath, and yet persisting. The concept of alterlife came out of efforts to grapple with the transgenerational injurious effects of industrially produced chemicals now ubiquitous in the atmosphere and water, some of which, like PCBs and DDE (a metabolite of DDT), appear to be in the bodies of every person alive on the planet. I come to alterlife after studying these chemicals as they deliver concentrated injury and premature death to already assaulted communities, and also continue spreading ubiquitously across the earth, transforming the epigenomes, neurobiology and metabolisms of living beings, human, non-human, and more than human.

Since 2001 when the CDC began national biomonitoring studies in the US, other endocrine disrupting chemicals, like phthalate plasticizers, dioxins, furan, lead, and organochlorine pesticides, and organophosphate pesticides have joined PCBs and DDT in the bodies of all people tested. In Canada, lead and mercury are near universally in bodies, even as we know, from both science and communities, that the violence of these chemicals is concentrated in Indigenous territories, such as Grassy Narrows and Aamjiwnaang First Nations. Such pollution is a persistent form of colonial violence, an interruption to Indigenous sovereignty and the relations that make up land and life. Thinking alterlife is an ongoing project, and thus what I can offer here are invitations and openings, rather than summations, towards making a concept in support of a distributed reproductive politics.

Alterlife has become a political concern for me as I live as a guest in Tkaronto/Toronto, on Anishinaabe territories, on the Great Lakes governed by the Dish and One Spoon Wampum Treaty, and in Canada, a settler colonial and petro-extraction state. The question of alterlife is shaped by a sense of responsibilities as a guest of this place, to its water and land, to its knowledge-making, and to my own position as an urban Métis person from Winnipeg with responsibilities to both my complicities in settler colonialism and whiteness as well as activations of decolonial Indigenous relations. To be a white-coded Métis in settler colonial spaces is to be messily pulled between systems intent on Indigenous erasure interconnected with structures of white entitlement.

Alterlife is a concern here in Canada, where entangled relations of life and death take the form of neoliberal managerial governance combined with a capitalist settler colonial extraction regime that together create a potent environmentally violent mix dependent on Indigenous dispossession. Alterlife is a concern for me as someone who lives with bodies of water that hold 21% of the world's fresh surface water, and 84% of North America's. Alterlife is a concern for me as I live as a guest of both ancestors and those yet to come, who also already have relations with this land. Thus, my thinking of alterlife is also about upholding Indigenous sovereignties and continuing Land/Body relations in the ongoing aftermaths of settler colonialism, even while surrounded by skyscrapers and enmeshed in the enjoyments and densities of city life.

My sense of a politics of distributed reproduction for the condition of alterlife is also animated by emergent technoscientific renderings of endocrine disruption and metabolism that overflow the old singular toxicological focus on acute poisonings that have previously been used to map (and limit) the terrains of environmental violence. Some scientists are now tracking low dose epigenetic, neurobehavioral, developmental, and metabolic effects of industrial chemicals, some of which may be transgenerational. What it means to be a human is to materially develop in the uneven distribution of chemical exuberances of a century of industrial capitalism. *As such, the very premise of the discrete body is unravelling.* Microbiome research, for example, shows how bodies are not singular organisms, but instead always collectivities. These are emerging research trajectories that might be collaborated with towards thickening a sense of alterlife.

Moreover, Hannah Landecker has identified a turn to a "post-industrial metabolism" in which many life scientists now explicitly acknowledge that their object of inquiry has become life forms that are materially transformed at biochemical registers by entanglements with a capitalist-made built environment both inside and outside labs. The nascent field of "exposomics" likewise extends the sense of the beings and doings that make up bodies by attending to the metabolic effects of synthetic chemical exposures as they accumulate and cause metabolic changes in bodies from conception onward. While this field is aimed at creating a personalized medicine that can address the problematics of individual exposure, it nonetheless sparks a potential for new ways of studying exposures as the extensive molecular alteration of life in capitalist fields of relation.

To these emerging fields of research, environmental epigenetic studies are now suggesting that the environments of our ancestors may be present inside us as *inherited metabolic patterns*. This bundle of research contributes towards a sense of relational living-being that extends not only outward into multi-species and land relations, but out into the very physical infrastructures of capitalism, colonialism, and racism. Or put another way, it offers a sense of how such infrastructures are physically present inside of us, unevenly distributing harms and supports. These are not the life forms of cold war population models. They point to different kinds of densities and relations of becoming. While evocative, these various technoscience materializations of the already-altered body need to be troubled, challenged, collaborated with, and recomposed with critical research from Black studies, Indigenous studies, postcolonial studies, queer studies, and trans studies, fields that have many lessons for how to craft concepts, existences, kinships, and political actions that rise from and resist the aftermaths of structural violence. Alterlife is forged in recognition of the long duration of densified everyday environmental violence. Alterlife does not happen at the scale of molecules, it is extensive, now planet wide, even as it is unevenly concentrated in some places and bodies.

Learning from and making kin with the decolonial projects of Frantz Fanon, Sylvia Wynter, and Indigenous Land/body prophecies, understanding the densities that make up "alterlife" is a project aimed at summoning new forms of humanity, not preserving the human that histories of deep violence have created. Alterlife is not waiting for the apocalypse—apocalypses of many kinds have already happened, even as livable worlds keep being snatched away. First the buffalo, then the land, now the water. Alterlife resides in what Frantz Fanon called "an atmosphere of certain uncertainty." This is a crucial point. The frame of population crisis and the Anthropocene both put apocalypse on the horizon. It is yet to come. This is telling. For whom has massive violence not already been a daily struggle, and thus who has the luxury to think endangerments to life are in the future? Alterlife, in contrast, insists on a different temporality, recognizing the many long-standing world-destructions, from settler colonialism to plantation slavery. As Kyle Whyte argues, Indigenous people of Turtle Island already know well loss of land—through land theft, displacement, and industrialism—and do not have to wait for climate change to intimately know forms of loss tied to land change. Slavery too brutally robbed people of their worlds, their lands, their knowledges, languages, and relations, creating legacies of dehumanization and death, as well as accumulations of wealth out of unfree labor, the structures of which are still at work today. Theorizing the plantation as an ongoing violence, Kathrine McKittrick asks, "What kind of future can the plantation give us?" In this spirit, the temporality of alterlife is one of the aftermaths, even as they are still happening, and for which there has been continual heterogenous projects of making life otherwise in the ongoing fallout.

Of vital significance here is that life has not just been altered, it is more generally open to ongoing alteration, both desired and imposed, making and destroying, choreographed and unexpected. Alterlife resides in ongoing uncertain aftermaths, continuingly challenged by violent infrastructures, but also holding capacities to alter and be altered—to recompose relations to land and sociality, to love and sex, to survival and persistence, to undo some forms of life and be supported by others, to become alter-wise in the aftermath of hostile conditions, to surprise.

Alterlife is the condition of being already co-constituted by material entanglements with water, chemicals, soil, atmospheres, microbes, and built environments, and also the condition of being open to ongoing becoming. Hence, alterlife is already recomposed, pained, and damaged, but has potentiality nonetheless. If life holds together tensions between violence and possibility, braiding the organic and inorganic, body and land, and resides in the indistinctions between infrastructures and ecologies, recognizing Alterlife attends also to openness, to a potential for recomposition that exceeds the ongoing aftermaths. Refusing narratives of purity, or a sense of life as separate from its conditions, or a politics of reproduction separate from environment, alterlife strives for a politics of survival-as-resistance—what indigenous scholar Gerald Vizenor calls survivance. Alterlife is life damaged, life persistent, and life otherwise; life materialized in other ways and life exceeding our materializations.

The concept of alterlife is offered as a way of approaching the politics of relations in solidarity with the vast labors of anti-racist and decolonial reproductive and environmental justice activism, as well as Indigenous survivance and resurgence. This vision of decolonializing more-than-life collectivities draws inspiration from the work of many scholars, land defenders, activists, and artists, as well as students and friends, who are working hard to activate decolonial potentials now, without waiting for a better moment to arrive.

Core to the sense of alterlife is the acknowledgment that bodies are not separable from lands, waters, airs, and other non-human beings. Body defense is land defense, as the Native Youth Sexual Health Project's reproductive/environmental justice work teaches. The violences against the land, water, airs, and the many beings that are co-dependent on one another is also violence on bodies. "What happens to the land, happens to the people." Their recent campaign with Women's Earth Alliance on Land/Body Defense centers the experiences, resistances, and resurgences of Indigenous women, two-spirit, and young people whose lives are already also altered by racist colonial processes including the material environmental violence of extractive industries. There are generations of hard-earned learning to acknowledge and start from.

> Our current work cannot afford to forget that a movement for land/body defense has been growing consistently for many years; there are tools and strategies already tried and true or discarded. The first step, then, had to be talking to and honoring the knowledge of those grandmothers, mothers, aunties, and elders who most intimately know the relationship between body, place, people, and movement.

#LandBodyDefense. It is already here.

Those who benefit from oppressive systems have much work to do in calling forth alterlife, dismantling the work of whiteness in the ways environmental violence is structured with beneficiaries: the people and institution who are often densely supported and enriched by capitalist, colonial, and racist systems of consumption and waste. This teaching points to another way of conceiving of a politics of density. Where are the benefits of violence concentrated? Which density of enablement catches life in structures that demand environmental violence as the price of living? Most people are caught in quotidian and humble complicities that are entangled with the very acts of sheltering, eating, cleaning, and surviving that are in turn knotted to a cacophony of consumption and harms within supply chain capitalist webs, and tied to discard systems built into objects, tethering ordinary survival to the continual spewing of injury and persistent chemical violence.

Our relations are not just supportive, they can also be injurious and toxic. Vanessa Agard-Jones calls this "chemical kinship." Honoring "water is life" demands fraught practices of caring for bodies of water, geological processes, weather, and organisms, as well as relationships with the chemical and radioactive offspring born of extraction processes, nuclear power, and careful as well as careless discard. These non-innocent webs of relations are densified as white supremacy, multi-national corporations, and settler colonial nations. *They constitute the political problem of density; not human number counts of surplus life.* Métis artist and land defender Erin Marie Konsmo who works with Native Youth Sexual Health persistently reminds that an understanding of water as life includes queer, addicted, homeless, hungry, urban, and sick ways of being, and thus demands a politics of harm-reduction aimed at leaving none of our relations uncared for. No one is discarded because the land and water needs everyone. Attention to alterlife asks, not for a politics of fixing the other but, in the words of Fred Moten, "your recognition that it's fucked up for you, in the same way that we've already recognized that it's fucked up for us. I don't need your help. I just need you to recognize that this shit is killing you too however much more softly." Within the condition of alterlife the potential for political kinship and alter-relations comes out of the recognition of connected, though profoundly uneven and often complicit, imbrications in the systems that distribute violence.

One perversity of population control rhetoric today is that it focuses on places like Africa and Bangladesh, where everyday contributions to planetary environmental violence by humans is minimal. It worries about teenage Indigenous pregnancy in a world of settler colonial exterminations. It targets desperate displaced people passing over border fences looking for slightly better life chances. Population rhetoric points responsibility away from low-fertility, heteronormative, elite, massively consumptive lives that are profoundly supported by the exposure to structural violence of others. It deflects from the infrastructure of our current elite and human-centered support systems. It is this infrastructure that I want to attend to, built by a cosmology that frames the body as distinct and isolatable from conditions of becoming with the many. It is the result of seeing land as a resource, with bodies on it, rather than bodies as manifestation of land, and land as extensions of bodies.

Alterlife gathers at least three affirming gestures for a reconceptualized sense of more-than-life becoming within and against conditions of massive violence.

First, alterlife considers living-being within entanglements of becoming, and unbecoming, with others and infrastructures, as a project of future-making. What might a radically inclusive becoming-in-time together look like? No single being on this planet escapes entanglements with capitalism, colonialism and racism, even as their violent effects are profoundly concentrated in hotspots of hostility. Alterlife makes futures in explicit recognition and resistance to profoundly uneven distributions of life chances. Alterlife seeks to find other ways of persisting in ongoing aftermaths that materially redistribute densities of enablement and misery.

Second, alterlife thinks with and against ways of framing environmental violence in discourses about the Anthropocene (which tend to erase the complex histories that have generated and unevenly distributed environmental violence and benefits), as well as within scientific fields such as ecology, climatology, geology, demography, toxicology, epigenetics, and endocrine disruption that are riven by biopolitical grammars, challenging the ways damaged-based research redeploys portraits of racial and sexual difference and blame. Alterlife seeks to refuse the eugenic residual that calculates lives worth living, lives that are better not to have been born, lives not worth supporting, unproductive lives, and lives ignorable and killable. Such calculations vividly persist in policing, ecology, toxicology, demography, public health, economics and many other science, technical, and policy practices. Alterlife rejects damage-based research and biopolitical frameworks that focus the burden of representing violence (and hence the managerial aim and blame) on people, beings, and communities already confined in hostile worlds. Alterlife insists on a politics of valuing, loving, and supporting violated, endangered, and queer life, while fashioning problemizations and projects that attach responsibility to perpetrators and their infrastructures.

And **third**, alterlife compels speculation about futurity and potentials of being otherwise. Alterlife shares with responses to the Anthropocene a politics of non-deferral that is a commitment to act now. But this politics of non-deferral is not driven by the logic of the emergency, the scale of the planetary, or the container of the nation state. It is a politics of non-deferral interested in the humbleness of right here, in the scale of communities, and in the intimacies of relations.

Alterlife is a challenge to invent, revive and sustain decolonializing possibilities and persistances right now as we are, forged in non-innocence, learning from and in collaboration with past and present projects of resistance and resurgence. Thus, "Alterlife in the Ongoing Aftermath" is offered as an unfinished and ongoing call to collaborative action, land defense and reoriented responsibility. It is a calling forth of something else, even if that something is not known, even if small, and recognizing that this work has already been happening.

This version of hopefulness is not a deflection. Our bodies/lands are materialized through synthetic chemicals that bind to multinational corporations, through settler colonial extraction, through juridical systems that diminish the value of life and turn it into a cost benefit calculus for finance. I want to learn with others how to activate non-innocent, harm-reducing support systems that, here in Tkaronto, enact the radically generous potentials of Indigenous sovereignties and are mindfully responsible to our planetary relations. At the same time, I want to propagate responsibility to ongoing violences, the responsibility to not only build alter-relations, but also the responsibility to dismantle and shutdown. #AlterRelations and #ShutItDown.

Even as it dreams expansively, what this essay offers are some humble concepts derived from feminist decolonial STS as practiced on the Great Lakes, building on longer resistive legacies of Indigenous, Black, queer, and other projects of radical justice. Concepts that manifest environmental and reproductive justice together, that express Land/Body persistence in the ongoing aftermath. I can almost imagine a politics of alter-collectivities both more than pessimistic and less than optimistic, that draws from what was and what has persisted, that affirms, disrupts, dismantles, regenerates, and resists; a way of being oriented to relations and that cares about distributions, that needs new and old kinds of solidarities, interdisciplinarities, and pedagogies, and does not reproduce the same, that has concepts that grapple squarely with encompassing violences and yet propagate the alterwise. Almost. #AlterlifeintheAftermath

4

New Feminist Biopolitics in Ultra-low-fertility East Asia

Yu-Ling Huang and Chia-Ling Wu

In 2013, 37-year-old actress Jessie Chang made her first documentary, *Freeze My Eggs*, chronicling her reproductive adventures in Taiwan. To enhance her healthy body before the clinical procedures, this single woman went to see a doctor of Chinese medicine and a naturalist healer, quit smoking, and did yoga regularly. She then visited an assisted reproductive technologies (ART) center in Taipei and started her biomedical journey: testing her hormone levels, having ultrasounds to assess the quality of her ovaries, self-injecting an egg-stimulating drug for ten days, and undergoing egg-retrieval surgery under anesthesia. She then had fifteen eggs stored at a cost of NT $150,000 (roughly US $5,000) for the whole procedure. Taiwan's Artificial Reproduction Act allows only married couples to *access* ART. Thus, Jessie's plan, like other single women, was to freeze her healthy eggs while younger and use them when "Mr. Right" appeared. In her documentary, friends and relatives voice the pros and cons of her egg freezing. Some claim it is a woman's reproductive right and are full of praise for biological motherhood as a route to a fulfilling life; others encourage her to just find a man now and get married, opposing delayed motherhood. One interviewee argues that, given the detrimental effects of population growth, she cannot support the making of yet more babies.

Jessie's story illuminates the tensions around reproduction in an ultra-low-fertility country such as Taiwan. The fertility rate in East Asia has changed drastically. Not long ago, the region had one of the highest fertility rates in the world and was part of concerns about a "population bomb." Now, however, it has the lowest fertility rate globally. Taiwan, South Korea, and Japan have all slipped below the threshold of what demographers call the "ultra low fertility rate" of 1.4 children per woman. This is far below the "replacement rate" of 2.1 children, and even lower than China's actual fertility rate under the one-child policy (see Figure 1).

Even though the total population is still growing, worry about "overpopulation" has waned. Instead, anxiety about the "aging population" dominates. The drastic change is not only about not making babies; women (as well as men) are not even entering into marriage. In East Asia as a whole, the proportion of women aged 35–39 who have never married has reached an unprecedented high of twenty percent, and is even higher in Japan and Taiwan (see Figure 2).

All these countries are now calling the phenomenon of late marriage and low fertility a "crisis." One former president of Taiwan, Ma Ying-jeou, even framed it as a national security issue. And Japan established a new cabinet position, "Minister for Declining Fertility," to address the problem. Although these governments define low marriage and fertility rates as problems, public resources devoted to supporting families, such as child-care and housing for newly-weds, remain limited.

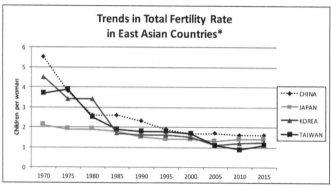

Figure 1: Raymo et al. 2015: 474.

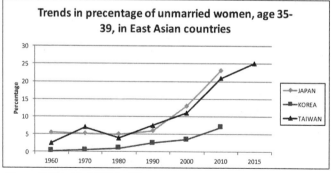

Figure 2: Trinidad 2015: 97.

Raymo and colleagues argue that the younger generation is either resisting marriage and everything that goes with it as less appealing, or is unable to afford to get married and raise children. Ochiai coined the concept of "familialistic individualization" to capture the paradox between the increase in single people and the enduring demands of personal responsibility for family in East Asia. She argues that familialism still dominates, and that when government responds to a crisis of social welfare caused by demographic change it tends to enact social reforms that reinforce and solidify the traditional family system.

To fight against such patriarchal measures aimed at countering late marriage and low fertility, feminists have been actively debating "social" policies such as maternity leave, childcare allowances, and more parent-friendly work structures and environments. Here we follow some of these feminist concerns, focusing especially on population science and reproductive technologies. Feminist STS perspectives center the importance of investigating technoscience to untangle biopolitics.

Not long ago, these countries made tremendous efforts, some coercive, in support of national family planning programs to reduce their fertility rates. Such population control strategies involved a lot of new knowledge-making and socio-technical networks, be it the IUD in Taiwan and South Korea, abortion in Japan, or sterilization in China. Feminist STS scholars have reflected on these programs, and their insights are equally important for non-natalism and pronatalism.

In this chapter, we seek to promote feminist biopolitics and call for new feminist agendas towards revisioning East Asia through three biopolitical goals. First, we seek to remake demography/population science by including women where they have previously been statistically excluded, especially but not only women as workers. Feminist demographers and others have generated excellent alternative frameworks which we briefly examine here.

Second, feminists seek to "seize the means of reproduction," and change laws and policies to better support women's reproductive autonomy individually *and* reproductive justice collectively, as well as enhancing family well-being. We note several recent developments vis-à-vis abortion, and subsidies for both contraception and infertility treatment.

Third, we urge the generation of more "緣-connected societies." While difficult to translate, this loosely means more innovative community-oriented social relations beyond one's family. New policies and living alternatives extend support to non-biologically related people. Such arrangements can substitute for families in their absence which, in these globalizing times, is increasingly the case. We provide several exciting examples. Making kin is sorely needed in East Asia, and it has begun.

Re-making Demography

Population science has shaped how we view the meanings of population and fertility for families, societies, and the planet. Scholars have called for remaking population science critically. While most policy-makers view ultra-low fertility in East Asia a serious problem, the scholarship challenges and complicates it with alternative viewpoints.

The first alternative is to integrate concerns about the environment, linking the issue of climate change with population dynamics. In post-war Asia, most technocrats followed Neo-Malthusians, investigating the adverse effects of population growth—food shortages, natural resource depletion, and lower standards of living—on overall economic development. They made serious efforts to reduce high fertility rates—the major negative factor believed to undermine a country's nascent industrialization. However, another group of economists regarded population growth, if developing a strong labor force, as positive for boosting economic productivity and consumption. In fact, the high economic growth rates in East Asia along with rapidly growing populations between 1960s and 1990s, called Malthus' principles fundamentally into question. For example, in the late 20th century, Taiwan was viewed as a fine example of making the best of a "demographic dividend" (when workers outnumbered dependents) to boost the nation's industrialization, gross national product, and per capita income.

Growing environmental degradation and carbon dioxide (CO_2) emissions in East Asia, particularly in China, have been associated with population growth. And today, China, Taiwan, and South Korea are among the worst ranked countries for environment performance, but still the governments often neglect environmental concerns in their population (and other) policy-making. Responding to the governments' strong pronatalist policies, a few environmentalists from East Asian countries asked that sustainability issue be taken into account. Unfortunately, policy makers have seldom done so vis-à-vis the low-fertility "crisis."

However, recent scholarship by Lutz and colleagues as well as by O'Neil and colleagues avoids simplistic causal links between population and environment, instead advocating creating new models to assess and build sustainable population policies. Concepts like "planetary health" are suggested to simultaneously reduce population growth, promote sustainable consumption, and redefine prosperity to include environmental health. Some scholars apply the Intergovernmental Panel on Climate Change (IPCC) model to incorporate different socioeconomic challenges to climate change into population projections.

The second alternative approach being pursued is re-conceptualizing aging and inter-generational relationships. The "crisis" of low fertility is often seen as connected to anxiety about the overall aging of the population. It is also related to how we assess economic development vis-à-vis population. Since the 1990s, economists and demographers have suggested the importance of taking an historical perspective on East Asia and attending to population composition (common demographic variables), dependency ratios (number of dependents per working person), and socioeconomic policies during the first demographic transition period in Taiwan (circa 1951–1984). Turning a low dependency ratio and a large number of young people into high labor force participation required a well-established infrastructure, high investment in human capital, *and* investment in social welfare policies.

In contrast, the low fertility rates and aging populations that have characterized East Asian and European societies during the past two decades have been expected to result in high dependency ratios, and some worrisome economic consequences. For example, according to the traditional population projections, the old-age dependency ratios in Taiwan and South Korea, currently around 20%, will approach 70% by 2050.

Some population scientists such as Lutz and colleagues offer alternative means of making such calculations. For example, instead of treating 65 years of age as the threshold of being elderly, some use remaining life expectancy years (such as 15 years or less) as the new indicator of "being old." Using this new indicator, the aging population increases much less than with the conventional calculation.

Others offer sophisticated models to reconsider the relationship between population composition, different age groups' economic activities, and the definition of "dependency." For example, economic demographer Ronald Lee and his colleagues in their 2014 *Science* article "Is Low Fertility Really a Problem?" offer new measurements to better capture *inter-generational relationships*. Using data from the National Transfer Accounts project that encompasses more than 60 countries, they estimated the value of goods and services produced and consumed by each age group and their intergenerational flows. They found that people's economic behaviors are changing: they are saving more for retirement and investing more in their children's education and other forms of human capital. Considering the macroeconomic implications of a changing population, Lee and colleagues proposed creating two new demographic summary measures: *the fiscal support ratio* (public transfers from taxpayers to beneficiaries), and *the support ratio* (private transfers from earners to consumers), which they argued should replace the conventional dependency ratio. Therefore, what aging means should not depend on the population composition but on the *supportive relationship between generations.* Kinship indeed!

Thirdly, some reformists' approaches highlight the importance of gender. Many argue that the empowerment of women through improved reproductive resources often leads to better wellbeing for the new born, the mother, and the family. Another important insight is to reconsider women's labor force participation in the age of low fertility. The traditional equation emphasizes the age and sex structure of the labor force; hence a society with a low fertility rate will soon face a shortage of workers. Yet some demographers suggest that factoring educational attainment into projections of labor force participation can more accurately demonstrate a qualitative dimension. This perspective is especially insightful within East Asian societies, where young women are highly educated but female labor force participation rates for age 15 and above hover around 50% due to women's "late entry" due to higher education and "early exit" due to marriage and childbirth.

In fact, the very conceptualization of the population "crisis" would be altered if the changing gender system were actually taken into account in the scenario, as many feminists are advocating. For example, Taiwanese demographer Yen-hsin Alice Cheng uses Sweden as an exemplar where a rise in fertility to replacement levels occurred when women were better integrated into the labor force. She uses the "Swedish scenario" for Taiwan's population projection: the workforce only diminishes slightly, and is composed of a woman-dominated labor force with high levels of education. Therefore, she joins other feminists and NGOs to argue that, to make the best of a future labor force with high per capita skill levels and productivity capacities, women as workers should be the focus of social policy reform. The government should provide more pro-family measures and more flexible labor force participation policies.

Recently more social scientists in East Asia such as Yip are now suggesting that we should adjust our mindset to living in a low-fertility society rather than seeking magic measures to produce a baby boom. Such a mindset would encourage reconsideration of the relationships between fertility, economy, and environment. Industry's technological inventions, as well as improvements in education, skills, and health among citizens, can increase labor force productivity and thereby offset shrinking population size to some extent, according to Yoshikawa. In addition, immigration policies and laws about foreigners working and creating families need to be more friendly and accepting, given how very much foreign workers and spouses have become vital parts of East Asian societies. Again, making kin.

Seize the Means of Reproduction

While the new demography questions whether low fertility is really a problem, governments in East Asia have launched various social policies to encourage marriage and childbearing. One worrying trend is the promotion of reproductive technologies for pronatalist purposes that may *both* threaten women's reproductive autonomy and create new health risks.

First, low fertility has become a rationale used by governments and conservative lawmakers to tighten access to abortion services. In South Korea, for example, abortion is against the law except in cases of rape or where the mother's health is endangered. Since the 1960s, however, illegal abortion has been widespread and has even become an important source of income for doctors. Governments have seldom enforced the law, reflecting an historical cultural understanding of abortion as a supplementary means to lower fertility in an overall national population control strategy. A recent *New York Times* article on the feminist push to end the ban noted, "For decades, the government's enforcement…has waxed and waned with the prevailing population trends." However, since 2009, the South Korean government has announced some "bold" steps to counter Korea's super low fertility rate, including re-enforcing the law to crack down on illegal abortion. In addition, some conservative doctors have started to echo calls for action. One group of doctors, for example, held a news conference in Seoul in 2010 to ask "forgiveness" for having performed illegal abortions. They formed a new organization, Pro-Life Doctors, which tries to discourage women from having abortions and runs a hotline to report clinics that perform them illegally.

In contrast, governments in countries such as Japan and Taiwan where abortion has been legal for health, ethical, and socioeconomic reasons cannot use such strict measures to limit abortion directly by law. They must use new methods. In Taiwan for example, abortion was legalized in 1984, partly due to the government's intention to further lower the fertility rate. Feminists also managed to voice a reproductive rights position within the discourse on privacy during the martial-law period. However, since the early 2000s, some legislators have proposed revising regulations on abortion to require a mandatory waiting period and consultation. Feminists and doctors have formed alliances to oppose such changes and, with such strong opposition, new regulations have not been passed. But the discussion did carve out a new discursive space for religious groups to voice anti-abortion rhetoric which had not previously appeared, even during the abortion legalization debates in the 1980s.

While changes to the abortion law have become a subject of lively public debate, according to Ha and to Chiang, cutting subsidy programs for contraceptive methods such as IUDs, sterilization, and vasectomy has attracted little attention in Taiwan and South Korea. Today only the poor and those with inherited diseases qualify for such financial support in Taiwan. In China, the government finally ended its one-child policy in 2015. One official measure of its new, two-child policy is to provide free IUD-removal surgery for women who experienced forced IUD-insertion. The story of such an insertion was vividly described in Nobel Laureate Mo Yan's novel *Frog*. Some Chinese, especially feminists, are angry about the new program, Wee reports, because the government again dares to recruit women's bodies for its new agenda before openly apologizing for its indecent one-child population policy that harmed thousands of women's reproductive health and autonomy.

A second new worrying trend is that assisted reproductive technologies (ARTs) have begun to gain governmental financial support, but there has been little public discussion of the health risks involved. Japan has offered partial subsidies of infertility treatments since 2004, South Korea since 2006, and Taiwan only since 2015. To boost the fertility rate, South Korea moved from partial financial support to fully incorporate ARTs under National Health Insurance coverage in 2017. One city government in Japan once provided public funds for single women to freeze their eggs in order to boost the declining birthrate. Although it has been debated whether such subsidies help increase the population, for the first time ART is now being linked with population growth, rather than being seen as solely a technical solution for infertility.

Among the various ART methods, single women's "social egg freezing" has been in the spotlight, as we illustrated with the story of actress Jessie Chang. Demand for egg freezing has increased rapidly in South Korea and Taiwan since the early 2010s, after a number of celebrities openly stated their desire to do so. The discourse of choice or reproductive autonomy dominates these discussions, as women "bank time" to preserve their eggs for anticipated infertility in their desire for later genetic motherhood. But compared with the benefits that ART clinics promote, the safety and efficacy of ARTs lack sufficient scrutiny. The procedures carry risks of ovarian hyper-stimulation syndrome and other complications.

Pregnancy and childbirth at later ages also involve greater health risks.

Since all of these East Asian countries allow only married couples access to ART, single women still need to wed "Mr. Right" in order to actually access and use their frozen eggs. Heteronormativity in terms of access to ART is not changing in East Asia. This partly explains why the actual use of frozen eggs to become pregnant remains quite low. In a more feminist analysis, it is also of questionable value to try to engage issues of reproductive autonomy using individual-focused strategies while neglecting the structural, social, and political reforms needed to genuinely expand women's reproductive options.

Overall, with the decline in fertility rates, new issues relating to what Murphy calls "seizing the means of reproduction" are arising—including in East Asia. While East Asian feminists have been cautious regarding new threats to abortion rights, there has been little feminist promotion of more liberalized use of ART, including surrogacy or access to sperm banks for single women. Instead, feminists in East Asia today struggle with the issues of compulsory motherhood and the medicalization of reproduction. Hence they would more likely promote use of reproductive technologies that control conception, and hesitate to use ARTs as enhancement technologies.

In sharp contrast, the LGBT communities in Taiwan and Japan are possibly the most vocal in seeking the right to access ARTs. Taiwan's Supreme Court ruled in favor of same sex marriage in May, 2017. With the foreseeable legalization of gay and lesbian unions, legal access to ART for LBGT people will likely become the next big reproductive justice battle for activists. Queer reproductive justice, rather than feminist-led women's reproductive rights, currently shapes the agenda in fighting against what Colen terms "stratified reproduction" in Taiwan.

Social Ties in Transition and 緣-Making

Demographic transitions have played a crucial role in molding East Asia's compressed modernity, and vice versa. The speed of both changing birth and death rates distinguished the first demographic transition in East Asia from that in the West. In their currently ongoing second demographic transitions, East Asian societies share some trends in marriage and family with Western societies, while also facing their own distinctive challenges. The first challenge is that marriage may no longer be considered an essential part of an individual's life course. In addition to later and fewer marriages and less frequent parenthood, a more dramatic trend in East Asia has been the increasing proportion of *both* men and women who remain single and childless despite society generally still valuing marriage.

The derogatory term "leftover women" (剩女 *shengnü*), used in China to refer to highly-educated women who are still single at the age of 27, became popular in 2007 and has even been promoted by state media. It exemplifies the stigmatization of female singlehood as it increases in frequency. In other parts of East Asia, the latest studies show emerging socioeconomic differences in marriage and divorce rates. For people in lower socioeconomic strata, marriage is becoming socially and economically expensive to seek and maintain. Economic recessions, long working hours, gender segregation in the workplace, and a preference for status homogamy in marriage can all reduce dating opportunities. In Western countries, sexual liberation has increased other forms of intimate relationships such as cohabitation, thus reducing the marriage rate. In contrast, East Asia has a quite different trajectory. In recent years, due to social, cultural and economic constraints, young people are being deprived of opportunities to develop long-term relationship in the first place.

The second challenge is that it has become harder in East Asia for families to perform their conventional functions. Since the Asian economic crisis of the late 1990s, people in Japan, Korea, and Taiwan, especially young adults, have suffered from continuing economic stagnation, worsening job insecurity, and diminished wage growth. Increasing recession and social inequalities not only keep more people from marriage, but also limit their economic independence. Yet despite changing family formations born of global economic decline, governments still rely on "familialization policies" that seek to maintain the family as the unit of welfare to take care of its members by itself or through the market. People without family, or whose families fail to provide, can be quite marginalized in terms of economic support as well as social connections.

Two distinctive problems are emerging from these failing policies. First, more young adults live with their parents, while unmarried middle-aged and elderly people often live alone and have no one to depend on. In 1999, Japanese sociologist Masahiro Yamada coined the controversial phrase "parasite single" (パラサイト・シングル *parasaito shingeru*) to describe the tendency of adult children to live with their parents into their thirties.

Second, single person households provide fewer social supports, especially but not only in old age. For example, the 2010 NHK documentary *Muen Shakai* (無縁社会, the 'no-relationship society') found that each year 32,000 people died alone in Japan with no, or only weak, social ties, and for whom officialdom might have no one to whom to even issue a death certificate. Such "invisible" deaths indicate deeply changing family structures in Japan, and the bleak consequences of social isolation.

Organizing new social ties beyond those of the traditional family is becoming an important challenge in East Asian societies. Research that compares married and unmarried people's well-being in the West suggest that being single does not necessarily lead to social isolation if people can maintain family relations and also establish steady interpersonal networks with friends, co-workers, and other types of "weak" (i.e., "non-familial") social ties. To most East Asians, given that the traditional family bonds on which they used to rely are crumbling and their chances of finding a partner are decreasing, finding new ways to build social connections is becoming urgent.

Feminists have recognized the solidarity of women based on shared conditions, experiences, and concerns, over and above biological bonds. Ueno Chizuko, a prominent feminist in Japan, published a guide for an active and happy life for older women (and later another guide for men as well) who have been or become single through divorce, widowhood, or never having married. Both books became best sellers in Japan. Although this proposed lifestyle has been criticized as financially affordable only by the middle and upper classes, innovative ideas for creating social lives beyond traditional family bonds are sorely needed.

The widely accepted East Asian cultural idea of "緣"—*en* (えん, in Japanese), *yuan* (緣, in Chinese) or *yeon* (연, in Korean)—*that congenial and understanding relationships between interdependent people can thrive both within and outside marriage and family*—offers a timely concept and social practice for making deep connections and diverse types of kin in our lives. Some rural communities in Japan have invented new ways to respond to their aging populations, such as home health care, and innovative arrangements to tie neighbors together. For example, "caregiver cafés," like 宮の森カフェ in Toyama Prefecture, were originally intended to provide a space for elders' family members to take a break from their caregiving labor. Now they have become a second home for children to play, young people to hang out, mid-life people to rest, and all to find a sense of belonging. A group of young Taiwanese physicians and NGOs are eager to introduce such care models to rural areas in Taiwan.

To create new social relations by re-arranging living spaces is another experiment happening as a response to the aging population, young working poor, unaffordable housing, and environmental sustainability. Local government and NGOs in northern Taiwan have initiated a co-living apartment project that invites elders and young people to live together. The shared kitchen, working area, and living room are spaces to hang out, eat, get to know each other, and to offer help when needed—like family members do.

Others are suggesting that strong *non-family ties* be taken more seriously and legally supported. Since 2012, the Taiwan Alliance to Promote Civil Partnership Rights has proposed amending the Civil Code, not only to legalize gay and lesbian marriage, but also to offer "families" consisting of non-blood-related persons (such as close friends) legal protections. This legal reform movement *to make friends into legal kin* has been heatedly criticized by conservatives, but it also opens up possibilities for designing new forms of intimate citizenship which are sorely needed.

Public cultures and technologies also offer bright ideas. Sociologist Yamada Masahiro observes that the younger generation in Japan has adopted the company of pets, a passion for animation, fandom, and commercial intimacy and sex, all to create a "virtual family" to fulfill the need of intimacy. A Japanese company designed the world's first holographic communication robot, a projected 3D animated girl inside an A4-size glass tube, as the perfect companion for hard-working single men. Targeting lonely salary men, the $2700 product promises that one's favorite animation character will greet you, reply warmly and promptly to your messages, and even do some tasks automatically such as turning on the lights before the "master" arrives home. While robots offer potential in addressing the desire for social interaction in Japan (and elsewhere), as feminists we must also be alert to the ways robots are often designed to reinforce conventional gender systems.

Taiwanese author Wu Ming-Yi in his award-winning novel *The Man with Compound Eyes* (2015) portrays a community on the east coast of Taiwan. There a widowed woman, a cat, aboriginal neighbors, butterflies, a young boy from a South Pacific island who has wandered to Taiwan through a trash vortex, and many other humans and non-humans, bond together for their life journeys. With the decline of blood ties and the degradation of nature resulting from capitalist development, reflective literature such as

Wu's work offers "a new way of telling our new reality," as feminist science fictionist Ursula Le Guin praised. Such work urges us to investigate new concepts, mindsets, and actions to revamp relations between population, economy, and environment while making new forms of kin. Ultra-low fertility can be regarded as a national security crisis, but it can also be a strong stimulant for a more en-connected new world.

5

Making Love and Relations Beyond Settler Sex and Family

Kim TallBear

Sufficiency
At a give-away—we do them often at pow-wows—the
family honors one of our own by thanking the People
who jingle and shimmer in circle. They are with us.
We give gifts in both generous show and as acts of faith
in sufficiency. One does not future-hoard. We may
lament incomplete colonial conversions, our too little
bank savings. The circle, we hope, will sustain. We
sustain it. Not so strange then that I decline to hoard
love and another's body for myself? I cannot have faith
in scarcity. I have tried. It cut me from the circle.
                                    The Critical Polyamorist

It was not always so that the monogamous couple ideal
reigned. In *Public Vows: A History of Marriage and
Nation*, Nancy Cott argues that in the US the standard
of lifelong monogamous marriage took hold in the
19th century. It was propped up by Christian moral
arguments coupled with state structural enforcements

—the linking of marriage to property rights and notions of good citizenship.

In *Undoing Monogamy*, Angela Willey also shows how Christian mores regarding marriage and monogamy became secularized in late 19th-century scientific discourse. This is evident in the take-up of such standards by the US despite its stated commitment to a separation of church and state. Thus, marriage became central to supposedly secular US nation building that nonetheless assumed a culture of Christianity. In *The Importance of Being Monogamous*, Sarah Carter also shows how "marriage was part of the national agenda in Canada—the marriage 'fortress' was established to guard the [Canadian] way of life."

Growing the white population through biologically reproductive heterosexual marriage—in addition to encouraging immigration from some places and not others—was crucial to settler-colonial nation-building. Anthropologists Paulla Ebron and Anna Tsing argue in "Feminism and the Anthropocene" that heteronormative marriage and family forged through particular intersections of race, class, and gender worked to increase certain human populations and not others during rapid post-World War II colonial and capitalist growth of the US This "Great Acceleration" was extended globally and involved systematic ecological and social destruction. Ebron and Tsing write, "White nuclear families anchored imagined 'safety' while communities of color were made available for sacrifice." Enclaves of white middle class spaces of safety were co-constituted with spaces of waste and ecological sacrifice, what Ebron and Tsing, after Traci Brynne Voyles, call "wastelanding." Indeed, "Well-being was defined through the safety and security of well-ordered white families surrounded by specters of color, chaos and communism." In short, white bodies and white families in spaces of safety have been propagated in intimate co-constitution with the culling of black, red, and brown bodies and the wastelanding of their spaces. Who gets to have babies, and who does not? Whose babies get to live? Whose do not? Whose relatives, including other-than-humans, will thrive and whose will be laid to waste?

At the same time that the biologically reproductive monogamous white marriage and family were solidified as ideal and central to both US and Canadian nation building, Indigenous peoples who found themselves inside these two countries were being viciously restrained both conceptually and physically inside colonial borders and institutions that included residential schools, churches and missions all designed to "save the man and kill the Indian." If Indians could not all be killed outright—and persistent attempts were made to do so—then the savages might also be eliminated by forced conversions to whiteness. That is the odd nature of red as a race category in the US. In efforts to reduce numbers of Indigenous peoples and free up land for settlement, red people were viewed as capable of being whitened. As part of efforts to eliminate/assimilate Indigenous peoples into the national body, both the church and the state evangelized marriage, nuclear family, and monogamy. These standards were simultaneously lorded over Indigenous peoples as an aspirational model and used to justify curtailing their biological reproduction and steal their children.

So marriage was yoked together with private property in settler coercions of Indigenous peoples. The breakup of Indigenous peoples' collectively held-lands into privately-held allotments controlled by men as heads-of-household enabled the transfer of "surplus" lands to the state and to mostly European or Euro-American settlers. Cree-Métis feminist, Kim Anderson writes that "one of the biggest targets of colonialism was the Indigenous family," in which women had occupied positions of authority and controlled property. The colonial state targeted women's power, tying land tenure rights to heterosexual, one-on-one, lifelong marriages, thus tying women's economic well being to men who legally controlled the property. Indeed, women themselves became property.

Indigenous Relationality: e.g., Tiospaye, Oyate

One hundred and fifty-six years after the Dakota-US War of 1862, when my Dakota ancestors were brought under colonial control, the clearly unsustainable nuclear family is the most commonly idealized alternative to the tribal and extended family context in which I was raised. Prior to colonization, the fundamental social unit of my people was the extended kin group, including plural marriage. The Dakota word for extended family is *tiospaye*. The word for "tribe" or "people" (sometimes translated as "nation") is *oyate*, and governance happens in ways that demonstrate the connections between the two.

With hindsight, I can see that my road to exploring open non-monogamy began early in my observations in tribal communities of mostly failed monogamy, extreme serial monogamy, and disruptions to nuclear family. Throughout my growing up I was subjected by both whites and Natives ourselves to narratives of shortcoming and failure—descriptions of Native American "broken families," "teenage pregnancies," "unmarried mothers," and other failed attempts to paint a white, nationalist, middle class veneer over our lives. I used to think it was the failures to live up to that ideal that turned me off emphasizing domesticity, and that's why I ran for coastal cities and higher education, why I asserted from a very early age that I would never marry, nor birth children. Indeed, pregnancy was something I came to see as submitting to weakness that came with bleeding—with womanhood. It signified submission to men, What settler family did to my head!

But I was a happy child in those moments when I sat at my great-grandmother's dining room table with four generations, and later in her life with five generations. We gathered in her small dining room with its burnt orange linoleum and ruffled curtains, at the table beside the antique china cabinet, people overflowing into the equally small living room—all the generations eating, laughing, playing cards, drinking coffee, talking tribal politics, and eating again. The children would run in and out. I would sit quietly next to my grandmothers hoping no one would notice me. I could then avoid playing children's games and listen instead to the adults' funny stories and wild tribal politics.

Couples and marriages and nuclear families got little play there. The matriarch of our family, my great-grandmother, was always laughing. She would cheat at cards and tell funny, poignant stories about our family, about families and individuals—both Natives and whites—in our small town throughout the 20th century. Aunts and uncles would contribute their childhood memories to build on her stories. My mother would bring the conversation back to tribal or national politics. A great-grandchild might be recognized for a creative, academic, or athletic accomplishment. The newest baby would be doted on as a newly arrived human who chose our family. The Mom who might be 18 and unmarried would have help. As Kim Anderson explains in "Affirmations of an Indigenous Feminist":

> Our traditional societies had been sustained by strong kin relations in which women had significant authority. There was no such thing as a single mother, because Native women and their children lived and worked in extended kin networks.

Despite colonial violence against our kin systems, we are in everyday practice still quite adept at extended family. Beyond biological family, we also have ceremonies to adopt kin. And in my extended family we also engage in legal adoption. This is aided by the Indian Child Welfare Act (ICWA) that prioritizes the adoption of Native children by tribal families so children have a better chance of remaining inside tribal cultures. And it was Indigenous peoples ourselves who lobbied heavily for that legislation as one response to the colonial kidnapping of children of previous generations from Indigenous families who were impoverished by colonialism, and deemed unfit for not attaining the middle-class, nuclear family structures of white colonialists.

Compulsory Settler Sex, Family, and Nation

I did eventually marry—both legally and in a Dakota neo-traditional ceremony—when I was nearly 30. Despite my youthful disavowals, even I didn't have the oppositional momentum to jump the tracks of the marriage railroad. Today, I am nearly 50 and I see that it was not my family's so-called failures that dampened my enthusiasm for coupled domesticity. Rather, I was suffocating all my life under the weight of the aspirational ideal of middle-class nuclear family, including (hetero)normative coupledom with its compulsory biological reproduction, even while I had, it turns out, contentedly *lived* a counter narrative to that settler ideal for some years.

Unsurprisingly, the feeling of suffocation intensified after marriage and the pressure I felt to constitute a normative middle-class family. My co-parent is an anti-racist, feminist, Indigenous-rights-supporting, cisgendered white male who has mostly been the primary caretaker of our now teenager. I do not blame him as an individual for my misery in the marriage and nuclear family system. He did the best he could to help make a livable space for me. While I had no trouble bonding with my child as an individual human being, I could not shake my feeling of unease with the settler family structure, including its oppressive pronatalism.

Of course, there were babies born into my extended Dakota family. People have sex. Bodies beget life. But I did not see in my community a kind of pronatalism co-constituted with nation (state) building—an overture necessarily aimed at dispossessing Indigenous peoples of our human and other-than-human relatives. Instead, and I have only just now put words to this, I grew up with an implicit mandate that our tiospaye must caretake kin across the generations as part of caretaking the oyate, i.e. the "tribal nation" in 20th-century parlance. Some of our kin are born to us and some of them come to us in other ways. The roles of grandparents and aunties and uncles are revered as much as are mothers and fathers. I grew in a very pro-kinship world, but settler-state oppressions simultaneously sparked in me an explicit *non*natalism that is central to my rejection of the US nationalist project. If pronatalism involves reproducing the middle-class settler family structure, *no matter* the race or sexual orientation of the middle-class family, I lament it.

Kin-Making and Critical Nonmonogamy

Decolonization is not an individual choice. We must collectively oppose a system of compulsory settler sexuality and family that continues building a nation upon Indigenous genocide and that marks Indigenous and other marginalized relations as deviant. This includes opposing norms and policies that reward normative kinship ties (e.g., monogamous legal marriage, nuclear biological family) over other forms of kinship obligation. It includes living or supporting others in living within nonmonogamous and more-than-coupled bonds. It includes advocating policies that support a more expansive definition of family, and not rewarding normative family structures with social and financial benefits. Multiple scholars including Scott M. Morgensen and Katherine Franke show us how the present settler sexuality system attempts to railroad all of us into rigid relational forms established historically to serve the patriarchal heteronormative and increasingly also homonormative imperial state and its unsustainable private property interests and institutions.

Present-past-future: I resist a lineal, progressive representation of movement *forward* to something better, or movement *back* to something purer. I bring voices and practices into conversation from across what is called, in English, time. There are many lively conversationalists at my table—both embodied and no longer embodied. I lean in to hear them all in order to try and grasp ways of relating that Dakota people and other Indigenous peoples practiced historically. From what it is possible to know after colonial disruption to our ancestors' practices and our memories of how they related, marriage was different from relatively recent settler formations. Before settler-imposed monogamy, marriages helped to forge important Dakota kinship alliances but "divorce" for both men and women was possible. In addition, more than two genders were recognized, and there was an element of flexibility in gender identification. People we might call "genderqueer" today also entered into "traditional" Dakota marriages with partners who might be what we today consider "cisgendered." As I try to write this, I engage in essentially nonsensical conceptual time travel with categories that will lose their integrity if I try to teleport them back or forward in time. So much has gone dormant—will go dormant. So much has been imposed onto Indigenous peoples, both heteronormative settler sexuality categories and now also "queer" categories.

The record is also clear that there was plural marriage for men. What were/are the spaces for plural relations for and between women? An Indigenous feminist scholar from a people related to mine has confessed to me her suspicion that among our ancestors the multiple wives of one husband, if they were not sisters as they sometimes were, may have had what we today call "sexual" relations between them. She whispered this to me. As if we were blaspheming. But in a world before settler colonialism—outside of the particular biosocial assemblages that now structure settler notions of "gender," "sex," and "sexuality," persons and the intimacies among them were no doubt worked out quite differently.

Nathan Rambukkana, in his 2015 book *Fraught Intimacies: Non/Monogamies in the Public Sphere*, notes the potential of "queer or queered sexual or intimate relationships between sister- or co-wives." He cites a 2008 ethnography of a British Columbia Mormon community, Bountiful, in which two polygamist wives "married each other using Canada's same-sex marriage legislation." The two women "consider themselves life partners, although they have never explicitly discussed whether their relationship has a sexual component."

Recognizing possibilities of other kinds of intimacies—not focused on biological reproduction and making population, but caretaking precious kin that come to us in diverse ways—is an important step to unsettling settler sex and family. So is looking for answers to questions about what intimacies were and are possible beyond the settler impositions we now live with. These are formidable tasks that will be met with resistance by many Indigenous people. Our shaming and victimization, including in "sexual" ways, has been extreme. The imposition of Christianity has ensured that speaking of and engaging in so-called sexual relations in the ways of our ancestors was severely curtailed. Our ancestors lied, omitted, were beaten, locked up, raped, grew ashamed, suicidal, forgot. We have inherited all of that. And we have inherited Christian sexual mores, and settler state biopolitics that monitor, measure, and pathologize our bodies and our peoples, including forcibly sterilizing Indigenous women. Yet they've also promoted heteronormative biological reproduction (for some, not all) as the only way to make babies and kin.

With that history as the cliff looming above us, it is no small thing to ask Indigenous thinkers to turn their decolonial lenses towards a critique of normative marriage and family formations that many of us now aspire to. It is no small request to ask Indigenous people to consider the advantages of open nonmonogamy, with a community's knowledge and partners' consent as an important decolonial option. For now, few will have that choice. I suspect there are especially younger Indigenous people who might join me in thinking hard on the nonmonogamous arrangements of our ancestors. We are so keen to embrace other decolonizing projects—to consider the wisdom of our ancestors' ways of thinking. Why should we not also consider nonmonogamous family forms in our communities?

I have had especially white feminists bristle at my refusal to condemn Dakota historical practices of plural marriage. How can I support "polygamy"—with that word for them meaning one man with several wives? It can also refer to one woman with multiple men. These women's views on nonmonogamy are conditioned by their impressions of nonconsensual or not rigorously consensual forms of nonmonogamy in which men alone have multiple wives. They often cite Mormon or Muslim polygamies. I can't speak with much expertise to the variety of nonmonogamous practices among those peoples, although I know that there are varying levels of consent and not all polygamy should be painted with the same broad brush. But I ask us, as Indigenous people, to learn what we can about the role of nonmonogamy in our ancestors' practices, which, importantly, were not often attached to prose-lytizing religions, and which normatively featured greater autonomy for women. What I know of my ancestors is that women controlled household prop-erty. And marriage did not bind them to men econom-ically in the harsh ways of settler marriage.

What were the values underlying our ancestors' nonmonogamy that might articulate with 21st-century Indigenous lives? Many Indigenous communities still exhibit a framework of extended kinship where respon-sibilities are more diffusely distributed, where we work as groups of women (or men, or other gendered people ideally) to share childcare, housing, and other resources. In my experience, our ways of relating often seem to contradict the monogamous couple and nuclear family. I am interested in seeing us not only implicitly but also explicitly de-center those family forms. Perhaps our allegiances and commitments are more strongly conditioned than we realize by a sense of community that *exceeds* rather than *fails to meet* the requirements of settler sex and family. The abuse and neglect in so many Indigenous families born of colonial kidnapping, incarceration, rape, and killing are all too real. But perhaps our relentless moves to caretake in *tiospaye* more than in normative settler family forms is not simply the best that we can do. Maybe it is the best way to heal?

I've seen sociological research under the label of Indigenous Masculinities—pro-Indigenous father-hood research—that centers the normative two-parent, nuclear family form without question. Colonial notions of family insidiously continue to stigmatize us as they represent the normative standard against which we are measured. Perhaps our kinship arrangements are actually culturally, emotionally, financially, and environmentally more sustainable than that nuclear family, two-parent model we are so good at failing at, and that's why we are "failing."

If we already often share children, economic sustenance, and housing, why must sex be reserved for the monogamous couple, or for making babies? Sexual monogamy can in one interpretation be seen as hoarding another person's body and desire, which seems at odds with the broader ethic of sharing that undergirds extended kinship. What if my colleague's suspicion is correct? Is it so uncomfortable to imagine women, in partnership also with the same husband (with everyone's gender identification more complex than biology alone)—sharing not only say daily work, but also, when the need or desire arose, sharing touch as a form of care, relating, or connection?

Disaggregating Sexuality and Spirituality: Reaggregating Relations

> Sexuality is not "like" power...sexuality is a form of power: and, of the forms of power, sexuality in particular might prove uniquely efficacious in both individual and collective healing. Further, I will suggest that sexuality's power might be forceful enough to soothe the pains of colonization and the scars of internal colonization.
>
> David Delgado Shorter

In an essay entitled simply, "Sexuality," Indigenous Studies scholar David Shorter focuses on *moreakamem* —healers, seers, powerful people among the Yoeme, an Indigenous people living on both sides of the Mexico/US border. He originally set out to understand the "spiritual" aspects of what they do—to examine *moreakamem* as powerful healers—but his research revealed entanglements of both "sexuality" and "spirituality." During his fieldwork with southern Yoeme in Sonora, Mexico, an elder told Shorter that individuals who engage in nonmonogamous and/or non-heterosexual relationships are commonly also *moreakamem*. This is not always the case, but it is often the case. In fact, in northern Yoeme communities in Arizona, *moreakame* has come to be conflated with terms such as "gay," "lesbian," or "two-spirit," and other less positive terms. The healer or seer aspect of the word has by now been lost among Yoeme living in the US, who have much ethnic overlap with "Catholic Mexican American" communities.

Shorter found that he could not understand the powerful "spiritual" roles in community of *moreakamem* without also understanding their so-called sexualities. Shorter explains that in many Indigenous contexts, there is an "interconnectedness in all aspects of life." So following the connections between sex and spirit among the Yoeme was akin to "following a strand of a spider's web." In English we are accustomed to thinking of "spirituality" or "spirit," "sexuality" or "sex" as things, and as assuredly separate things. With that ontological lens *moreakamem* become an object, a class of person defined along either sexual *and/or* "spiritual" lines. However, within their context, sexuality and spirituality can both be seen as actually constituted of "human relational activities." They are sets of relations—through which power is acquired and exchanged in reciprocal fashion among persons, not all of them human. In describing how relations or the relational sharing of power become things in a non-Indigenous framework, Shorter uses the term "objectivating the intersubjective." In another simply titled essay, "Spirituality," he explains that "'Intersubjective,' like 'related,' emphasizes mutual connectivity, shared responsibility, and interdependent well-being." So we might think of sexuality, spirituality, and nature too as not things at all, but as sets of relations in which power (and sometimes material sustenance?) circulates. We might resist objectivating the intersubjective. We might resist hardening relations into objects, which might make us more attuned to relating justly in practice.

To return to *moreakamem* and resisting a classification of them as gay, or nonmonogamous, we can see them instead as relating. They have reciprocity with and receive power in their encounters with spirits, ancestors, dreams, animals. And also in the human realm when they use their power to see for and heal other humans suffering from love or money problems, addictions, and other afflictions of mind and body.

Emphasizing relations and exchange, Shorter explains that the "social role of 'moreakamem'" is not "a means for individual self-empowerment." A *moreakame* does not identify themselves as such. Although we do so identify them in order to refer to them. *Moreakamem* do not accentuate their pertinent personal characteristics and capacities, i.e., their "sexuality" or their power to heal. Shorter explains that *moreakamem* focus rather on their work in community, that they "work tirelessly and selflessly to maintain right relations." They resist having their relational activities and power objectified.

Understanding *moreakamem* relationality in community helps us to understand their so-called sexuality (and ours too) as a form of reciprocity and power exchange. We can begin to unthread it from being an object like "gay" or "straight" that is "constituted once and unchanging." So-called sexuality is one form of relating and sharing of power that is "reconstituted over and over based on the intersubjective dynamism of two or more persons." Shorter encourages us to see that for *moreakamem*—and for all of us—"sexuality" can be understood "as a way of being that...directly and intentionally mediates social relations across the family, clan, pueblo, tribe, and other forms of relations including other-than-human persons." With this understanding, sexuality beings to look "more like a type of power, particularly one capable of healing."

David Shorter does not reveal the details of *moreakamem* sexual relations beyond noting their often non-normative sexualities. But his theoretical treatment of sexuality as relational power exchange is instructive for pondering how Indigenous people (and others) might find ways in collectivity to oppose settler sexuality and marriage. Given the goal of thinking relationally, what might "indigenizing sexuality" mean? I hope it is clear by now that the question is actually oxymoronic. Rather, we might consider that the goal is to disaggregate so-called sexuality not back to tradition, not forward into progress, but into and back out into that spider's web of relations. (Or any net visual that works for you.) That is a web or net in which relations exchange power, and power is in tension, thus holding the web or community together.

So this is my thought experiment: As part of decolonial efforts can we work ourselves into a web of relations (I am thinking in terms of space and not a time concept now). In small moments of possibility, can we resist naming "sex" between persons and "sexuality" as nameable objects? Can such disaggregation help us decolonize the ways in which we engage other bodies intimately—whether those are human bodies, bodies of water or land, the bodies of other living beings, and the vitality of our ancestors and other beings no longer or not yet embodied? By focusing on actual states of relation—on being in good relation-with, making kin—and with less monitoring and regulation of categories, might that spur more just interactions?

We could do the same thought experiment with "spirituality" too for it is also about relationality and engaging other bodies, maybe just not always material ones. We won't escape the moments when "sex" or "sexuality," "spirit" or "spirituality" are the best we can do with this limited English language. But can we lean toward disaggregating objects and instead focus on promiscuously reaggregating relations? Can we see ourselves as relating and exchanging power and reciprocity in support of a stronger *tiospaye* or extended kin network with both living relations and those whose bodies we come from, and whose bodies will come in part from us? I am thinking of both the human and other-than-human bodies with whom we are co-constituted.

Many other scholars of "Native American" history or Indigenous Studies have written key texts that inform my evolving thinking on the issues discussed in this chapter. Influential historians include Philip Deloria, Theda Perdue, and Brian Dippie. Also influential are race scholars who do the rarer work of accounting for the intersections of race and Indigeneity. These include scholars such as Circe Sturm, Cheryl Harris, Aileen Moreton-Robinson, Jenny Reardon, Eve Tuck, and Yael Ben-zvi. Their work is listed in the References and the online Sourcenotes.

Conclusion

To return to the by now mundane topic of nonmonogamy, in relating with more than one partner in my life, I have come to regularly ponder how this serves kinship across my life. How do these relations serve others? What about our respective children? Multiple "romantic" relations can help raise and mentor children in community. How do our relations serve our other partners? I have found affectionate and supportive friendship with partners of my partners. This is a key benefit for me of open nonmonogamy. How does the different sustenance I gain from multiple lovers collectively fortify me and make me more available to contribute in the world? If I am richly fed, what and who am I able to feed? What is possible with a model in which *love* and *relations* are not considered scarce objects to be hoarded and protected, but which proliferate beyond the confines of the socially constituted couple and nuclear family?

What began as a personal political experiment in open nonmonogamy is turning to de-emphasizing monogamy *and non*monogamy as objectified forms of "sexuality." I am also indebted to fellow feminist science studies scholar, Angela Willey, for inspiring my newly established will to unsettle both concepts. I am caught up sometimes in objectivating the intersubjective, that is, when I identify myself as "nonmonogamous"—as a sort of form of sexuality. Let me be clear, that I view open nonmonogamy as but one step in a process of decolonizing from compulsory settler sexuality. It is a placeholder until I/we find other ways of framing and naming more diffuse, sustainable and intimate relations.

As an Indigenous thinker, I am constantly translating. I see Indigenous thinkers across the disciplines and outside of the academy doing similar work— combining our fundamental cultural orientations to the world with new possibilities and frameworks for living and relating. Our peoples have been doing this collectively in the Americas for over five centuries, translating, pushing back against colonial frameworks, and adapting them. We've done it with respect to syncretic forms of religion and ceremony, with dress, music, language, art and performance. Why should we not also articulate other ways to lust, love, and make kin? A de-objectified reconstituting of right relations, and nurturing, healing exchanges of power seem an important next step. Within the grand scheme of things, purposeful and open nonmonogamy, and reconceiving of more just intimacies with other-than-humans seem like important next steps.

In conclusion, I return to my *tiospaye* and to Indigenous peoples, I no longer see our failures at lasting monogamy and nuclear family as failure. From where I stand it looks like most of my extended family members have more security in our small town tribal community or in the "urban Indian" community in which I spent part of my childhood, than they do in Euro-centric traditions of nuclear family and marriage. I see us deep inside the shifting walls of this colonial edifice that took most of the world's resource to build, experimenting and working incrementally with tools and technologies that we did not craft. I see us combining these with Indigenous cultural templates in any open space we can find to build lives and communities of relations that make any sense to us at all. ◼

References

Acquaye, Alisha. 2017. "Black to the Future: OkayAfrica's Introduction to AfroFuturism." *OkayAfrica*, 10 July. Available at: http://www.okayafrica.com/african-future-okayafrica-introduction-afrofuturism/ (accessed 10 January 2018).

Adams, Carol and Josephine Donovan, eds. 1995. *Animals and Women: Feminist Theoretical Explorations*. Durham: Duke University Press.

Adams, Vincanne. 2012. "The Other Road to Serfdom: Recovery by the Market and the Affect Economy in New Orleans." *Public Culture*, 24, n. 1, pp. 185–216.

"Afterlife." n.d. Available at: Merriam-Webster.com (accessed 3 January 2018).

Agard-Jones, Vanessa. 2013. "Bodies in the System." *Small Axe*, 17, n. 3 (42), pp. 182–92.

—. 2014. "Spray." *Somatosphere*. Available at: http://somatosphere.net/2014/05/spray.html (accessed 28 July 2016).

Akhter, Farida. 1992. *Depopulating Bangladesh: Essays on the Politics of Fertility*. Dhaka: Narigrantha Prabartana.

Almeling, Rene. 2011. *Sex Cells: The Medical Market for Eggs and Sperm*. Berkeley: University of California Press.

—. 2015. "Reproduction." *Annual Review of Sociology*, 41, pp. 423–442.

Anderson, Kim. 2010. "Affirmations of an Indigenous Feminist." In Cheryl Suzack, Shari M. Huhndorf, Jeanne Perreault, and Jean Barma, eds., *Indigenous Women and Feminism: Politics, Activism, Culture*, pp. 82–91. Vancouver and Toronto: UBC Press.

Angier, Natalie. 2013. "Families." *New York Times*, 26 November, *Science Times* section: D1–D8.

Anway, Matthew D. and Michael K. Skinner. 2006. "Epigenetic Transgenerational Actions of Endocrine Disruptors." *Endocrinology*, 147, n. 6, pp. S43–S49. Available at: https://doi.org/10.1210/en.2005-1058 (accessed 13 January 2018).

Asian Communities for Reproductive Justice. 2005. "A New Vision for Advancing Our Movement for Reproductive Health, Reproductive Rights, and Reproductive Justice." Available at: https://forwardtogether.org/wp-content/uploads/2017/12/ACRJ-A-New-Vision.pdf (accessed 15 January 2018).

Bailey, Moya and Ayana Jamieson. 2017. "Introduction: Palimpsest in the Life and Work of Octavia E. Butler." *Palimpsest: A Journal on Women, Gender, and the Black International*, 6, n. 2, pp. v–xiii.

Bailey, Moya and Whitney Peoples. 2017. "Towards a Black Feminist Health Science Studies." *Catalyst: Feminism, Theory, Technoscience*, 3, n. 2. Available at http://catalystjournal.org/ojs/index.php/catalyst/article/view/120/pdf_14 (accessed 9 January 2018).

Baldwin, Kylie, Lorraine Culley, Nicky Hudson and Helene Mitchell. 2014. "Reproductive Technology and the Life Course: Current Debates and Research in Social Egg Freezing." *Human Fertility*, 17, n. 3, pp. 170–179.

Barker, Joanne, ed. 2017. *Critically Sovereign: Indigenous Gender, Sexuality, and Feminist Studies*. Durham, NC: Duke University Press.

Barker, Joanne. 2017. "The Seeders." Available at: https://joannebarkerauthor.com/2017/05/10/the-seeders/ (accessed 3 January 2018).

Barry, Ellen and Suhasini Raj. 2014. "12 Women Die After Botched Government Sterilizations in India." *New York Times*, Nov. 12:A4.

—. 2014. "Indian State Recalls Pills Linked to Sterilization Deaths." *New York Times*, Nov. 15:A7.

Bashford, Alison. 2014. *Global Population: History, Geopolitics, and Life on Earth*. New York: Columbia University Press.

Bashford, Alison and Joyce E. Chaplin. 2016. *The New Worlds of Thomas Robert Malthus: Re-reading the Principle of Population*. Princeton, NJ: Princeton University Press.

Becker, Gary. 2007. "Human Capital." In David R. Henderson, ed., *The Concise Encyclopedia of Economics. Library of Economics and Liberty*, 2nd ed. Available at: http://www.econlib.org/library/Enc/HumanCapital.html (accessed 1 January 2018).

Beliso-De Jesus, Aisha M. 2015. *Electric Santería: Racial and Sexual Assemblages of Transnational Religion*. New York: Columbia University Press.

Bell, Ann V. 2014. *Misconception: Social Class and Infertility in America*. New Brunswick, NJ: Rutgers University Press.

Bell, Susan E. 2003. "Sexual Synthetics: Women, Science and Microbicides." In Monica J. Casper (ed.) *Synthetic Planet: Chemical Politics and the Hazards of Modern Life*, pp. 197–212. New York: Routledge.

—. 2009. *DES Daughters, Embodied Knowledge, and the Transformation of Women's Health Politics in the Late Twentieth Century*. Philadelphia, PA: Temple University Press.

Bell, Susan E. and Kathy Davis. 2017. "'Historical Fragments' Mobile Echo: Encountering the Current Refugee Crisis with Ai Weiwei." *Transfers*, 7, n. 2 (Summer), pp. 115–119.

Benjamin, Ruha. 2013. *People's Science: Bodies & Rights on the Stem Cell Frontier*. Palo Alto, CA: Stanford University Press.

—. 2016. "Racial Fictions, Biological Facts: Expanding the Sociological Imagination through Speculative Methods." *Catalyst: Feminism, Theory, Technoscience* 2, n. 2, pp. 1–28.

—. Forthcoming. *Race After Technology*. Cambridge, UK: Polity Press.

Benjamin, Ruha, ed. Forthcoming. *Captivating Technology: Reimagining Race, Resistance and Carceral Technoscience*. Durham, NC: Duke University Press.

Ben-zvi, Yael. 2007. "Where Did Red Go? Lewis Henry Morgan's Evolutionary Inheritance and U.S. Racial Imagination." *CR: The New Centennial Review*, 7, n. 2, pp. 201–229.

Bhattacharjee, Anannya, and Jael Silliman, eds. 2002. *Policing the National Body: Race, Gender and Criminalization in the United States*. Cambridge, MA: South End Press.

Blaser, Mario and Marisol de la Cadena. 2017. "The Uncommons: An Introduction." *Anthropologica*, 59, n. 2, pp. 185–93.

Bloom, David and J. G. Williamson. 1998. "Demographic Transitions and Economic Miracles in Emerging Asia." *The World Bank Economic Review*, 12, n. 3, pp. 419–455.

Bouse, Cortney Kiyo. 2014. "'Water, Water Everywhere': Racial Inequality and Reproductive Justice in Detroit." *Rewire*. 22 July 2014. Available at: https://rewire.news/article/2014/07/22/water-water-everywhere-racial-inequality-reproductive-justice-detroit/ (accessed 13 January 2018).

Bowker, Geof, Stefan Timmermans, Adele E. Clarke, and Ellen Balka, eds. 2015. *Boundary Objects and Beyond: Working with Susan Leigh Star*. Cambridge, MA: MIT Press.

Boyd, Zhaleh. 2017. "1800 and More: Mourning the Needy Dead in the Chaos of the Present." Talk delivered at Princeton African American Studies Graduate Student Conference, 20 April. Princeton, NJ.

Bradshaw, Corey J. A., Xingli Giam, and Navjot S. Sodhi. 2010. "Evaluating the Relative Environmental Impact of Countries." *PLOS ONE* 5, 3 May. Available at: http://journals.plos.org/plosone/article/file?id=10.1371/journal.pone.0010440&type=printable (accessed 16 January 2018).

Briggs, Laura. 2002. *Reproducing Empire: Race, Sex, Science, and U.S. Imperialism in Puerto Rico*. Berkeley, CA: University of California Press.

—. 2012. *Somebody's Children: The Politics of Transracial and Transnational Adoption*. Durham, NC: Duke University Press.

—. 2017. *How All Politics Became Reproductive Politics: From Welfare Reform to Foreclosure to Trump*. Berkeley, CA: University of California Press.

Brown, Adrienne Maree and Walidah Imarisha. 2015. *Octavia's Brood: Science Fiction Stories from Social Justice Movements*. Oakland, CA: AK Press.

Brown, Lester R. 2012. *Full Planet, Empty Plates: The New Geopolitics of Food Scarcity*. Rutgers University: Earth Policy Institute. Available at: http://www.earth-policy.org/books/fpep/fpepch1 (accessed 9 January 2018).

Buckley, Chris. 2015. "China Ends One-Child Policy, Allowing Families Two Children." *The New York Times*, 30 October. Available at: https://www.nytimes.com/2015/10/30/world/asia/china-end-one-child-policy.html?mcubz=0 (accessed 30 December 2017).

Burdette, Carolyn and Angelique Richardson. 2007. *Eugenics Old and New*. New Formations Series. London: Lawrence & Wishart.

Butler, Octavia E. [1979] 2004. *Kindred*. New York: Beacon Press.

Carbon Majors Database. 2017. "Carbon Majors Report."
London: Carbon Majors Database Worldwide. Available at:
https://b8f65cb373b1b7b15feb-
c70d8ead6ced550b4d987d7c03fcdd1d.ssl.cf3.rackcdn.com/
cms/reports/documents/000/002/327/original/ Carbon-
Majors-Report-2017.pdf?1499691240 (accessed 13 January
2018).

Carney, Molly. 2012. "Corrections Through Omniscience:
Electronic Monitoring and the Escalation of Crime Control."
Washington University Journal of Law and Policy, 40, n. 8, pp.
279–80.

Carpenter, Zoe. 2017. "What's Killing America's Black Infants?
Racism Is Fueling a National Health Crisis." *The Nation*,
February 15. Available at: https://www.thenation.com/
article/whats-killing-americas-black-infants/ (accessed 30
December 2017).

Carrington, Damien. 2014. "Earth Has Lost Half Its Wildlife in
the Last 40 Years, Says WWF." *The Guardian*, 29 September.
Available at: https://www.theguardian.com/
environment/2014/sep/29/earth-lost-50-wildlife-in-40-
years-wwf (accessed 21 December 2017).

Carter, Sarah. 2008. *The Importance of Being Monogamous:
Marriage and Nation Building in Western Canada to 1915.*
Edmonton: University of Alberta Press.

Casper, Monica J., ed. 2003. *Synthetic Planet: Chemical Politics
and the Hazards of Modern Life.* New York: Routledge.

Casper, Monica J. 2013. "Biopolitics of Infant Mortality."
Anthropologies, 17 (March). Available at:
http://www.anthropologiesproject.org/2013/03/
biopolitics-of-infant-mortality.html (accessed 29 December
2017).

Casper, Monica J. and Lisa Jean Moore. 2009. *Missing Bodies: The
Politics of Visibility.* NY: New York University Press.

@Cecilyk, Twitter post, 12/3/2014, 4:18pm. Available at
https://twitter.com/IAMYUNGJOC/status/540581050205
102080 (accessed 3 January 2018)

Chambers, Georgina M., Elizabeth A. Sullivan, Osamu Ishihara,
Michael G. Chapman, and G. David Adamson. 2009. "The
Economic Impact of Assisted Reproductive Technology: a
Review of Selected Developed Countries." *Fertility and
Sterility*, 91, n. 6, pp. 2281–2294.

Chan, Sewell. 2016. "Black Lives Matter Activists Protest Across Britain." *The New York Times*, August 6:A3.

Chen, Chao-Ju. 2014. "Producing the Right to Abortion: Legal Mobilization and Right Framing of the Women's Movement for the Legalization of Abortion in Martial-law Taiwan." *Academia Sinica Law Journal*, 15, pp. 1–76. (In Chinese: Chen, Chao-Ju. 2014. "Dazao duotaiquan jieyanqian duotaihefahua de fuyun falu dongyuan yu quanli goukuang." *Zhongyanyuan faxue qikan*, 15, pp. 1–76.)

Chen, Mel. 2012. *Animacies: Biopolitics, Racial Mattering, and Queer Affect.* Durham, NC: Duke University Press.

Cheng, Ling-Fang. 2015. "An Analysis of the Controversy over Proposed Revisions to Taiwan's Abortion Legislation in 2012." *Taiwan Journal of Public Health*, 34, n. 1, pp. 21–35. (In Chinese: Cheng, Ling-Fang. 2015. "2012 nian rengong liuchan xiufa zhengyi zhi fenxi." *Taiwan Weizhi*, 34, n. 1, pp. 21–35.)

Cheng, Yen-hsin and Elke Loichinger. 2015. "The Future Labor Force of an Aging Taiwan: The Importance of Education and Female Labor Supply." *Population Research and Policy Review*, 36, n. 3, pp. 441–466.

Cherel, Christina S. 2017. "Abortion without Provider Involvement: Exercising Autonomy Beyond Partisan Politics." *The Women's Health Activist: Newsletter of the National Women's Health Network* 42, n. 2 (March/April), p. 9.

Chiang, Sheng. 2013. "Abortion: Women's Rights, Obstacles, and Medical Ethics." *Formosan Journal of Medicine*, 17, n. 2, pp. 1–8. (In Chinese: Chiang Sheng. 2013. "Duotai: funu quanli, zhangai he yixuelunli." *Taiwan yixuehui zazhi*, n. 2, pp. 1–8.)

Children's Defense Fund. n.d. "Kinship Care Resource Kit for Community and Faith-based Organizations." Available at: http://www.childrensdefense.org/library/data/kinship-care-organization-resource-kit.pdf (accessed 3 January 2018).

Cho, Yu Fang. 2015. "Nuclear Diffusion: Notes Toward Reimagining Reproductive Justice in a Militarized Asia Pacific." *Amerasia Journal*, 41 (3), pp. 1–24. Available at: https://doi.org/10.17953/0044-7471-41.3.1 (accessed 13 January 2018).

Christopherson, Sarah. 2016. "NWHN-SisterSong Joint Statement of Principles on LARCS." *National Women's Health Network Newsletter*, 14 November, p. 9. Available at: https://www.nwhn.org/nwhn-joins-statement-principles-larcs/ (accessed 10 January 2018).

Clarke, Adele E. 1984, 1989. "Subtle Sterilization Abuse: A Reproductive Rights Perspective." In Rita Arditti, Renate D. Klein and Shelley Minden, eds., *Test Tube Women: What Future for Motherhood?* pp. 188–212. Boston: Pandora/ Routledge and Kegan Paul, 1st and 2nd eds.

—. 1995. "Modernity, Postmodernity and Human Reproductive Processes c.1890-1990, or 'Mommy, Where Do Cyborgs Come From Anyway?'" In Chris H. Gray, Heidi J. Figueroa-Sarrier, and Stephen Mentor (eds.), *The Cyborg Handbook*, pp. 139–156. New York: Routledge.

—. 1998. *Disciplining Reproduction: Modernity, American Life Sciences and the "Problem of Sex."* Berkeley, CA: University of California Press.

—. 2000. "Maverick Reproductive Scientists and the Production of Contraceptives c1915–2000." In Anne Saetnan, Nelly Oudshoorn and Myrja Kirejczyk, eds., *Bodies of Technology: Women's Involvement with Reproductive Medicine*, pp. 37–89. Columbus: Ohio State University Press.

—. 2008. "Introduction: Gender and Reproductive Technologies in East Asia." *EASTS: East Asian Science and Technology Studies: An International Journal*, 3, n.1, pp. 303–326.

Clarke, Adele and Teresa Montini. 1993. "The Many Faces of RU486: Tales of Situated Knowledges and Technological Contestations." *Science, Technology and Human Values*, 18, n. 1, pp. 42–78.

Clarke, Adele E. and Virginia Olesen, eds. 1999. *Revisioning Women, Health, and Healing: Feminist, Cultural and Technoscience Perspectives.* New York: Routledge.

Clarke, Adele and Alice Wolfson. 1990. "Class, Race and Reproductive Rights." In Karen Hansen and Irene Philipson, eds., *Women, Class and the Feminist Imagination: A Socialist-Feminist Reader*, pp. 258–267. Philadelphia, PA: Temple University Press.

Colaneri, Katie. 2016. "$3.5 Million Grant to Help Philly Cut Inmate Population, Launch Other Prison Reforms." WHYY, 13 April. Available at: http://www.newsworks.org/index.php/local/philadelphia/92812-35-million-grant-to-help-philly-cut-inmate-population-launch-other-reforms (accessed 3 January 2018).

Coleman, William. 1982. *Death Is a Social Disease: Public Health and Political Economy in Early Industrial France*. Madison, WI: University of Wisconsin Press.

Colen, Shellee. 1995. "'Like a Mother to Them': Stratified Reproduction and West Indian Childcare Workers and Employers in New York." In Faye Ginsberg and Rayna Rapp, eds., *Conceiving the New World Order: The Global Politics of Reproduction*, pp. 78–102. Berkeley, CA: University of California Press.

Co-living Apt. n.d. "Co-living Apt. Website." Available at https://www.9floorspace.com/sanxia (accessed 12 January 2018).

Collard, Rosemary Claire, Jessica Dempsey and Juanita Sundberg. 2015. "A Manifesto for Abundant Futures." *Annals of the Association of American Geographers*, 105, n. 2, pp, 322–330.

Collins, Patricia Hill. 1990. *Black Feminist Thought: Knowledge, Consciousness, and the Politics of Empowerment*. Boston, MA: Unwin Hyman.

—. 1999. "Will The 'Real' Mother Please Stand Up? The Logic of Eugenics and American National Planning." In Adele Clarke and Virginia Olesen, eds., *Revisioning Women, Health, and Healing: Feminist, Cultural and Technoscience Perspectives*, pp. 266–282. New York: Routledge.

—. 2008. *Black Feminist Thought: Knowledge, Consciousness and the Politics of Empowerment*. New York: Routledge.

Committee on Women, Population and the Environment (CWPE). 2001–2013. "Environment." Available at http://temp-cwpe.gaiahost.net/resources/environment (accessed 6 January 2018).

Conceivable Future. 2015–18. "Conceivable Future: Climate Crisis = Reproductive Justice Crisis." Available at: http://conceivablefuture.org/ (accessed 6 January 2018).

Connelly, Matthew. 2008. *Fatal Misconception: The Struggle to Control World Population*. Cambridge, MA: Harvard University Press.

Cott, Nancy. 2000. *Public Vows: A History of Marriage and Nation*. Cambridge, MA: Harvard University Press.

Crist, Eileen. 2016. "Choosing a Planet of Life." In Haydn Washington and Paul Twomey, eds., *A Future Beyond Growth: Towards a Steady State Economy*, pp. 43–55. London and New York: Routledge.

Crist, Eileen, Camilo Mora & Robert Engelman. 2017. "The Interaction of Human Population, Food Production, and Biodiversity Protection." *Science*, 356, 21 April, pp. 260–264.

Critical Polyamorist, The. 2018. "The Critical Poly 100s." Available at: http://www.criticalpolyamorist.com/critical-poly-100s.html (accessed 9 January 2018).

Crutzen, P.J. 2002. "Geology of Mankind." *Nature*, 415, p. 23.

Curtis, Bruce. 2001. *The Politics of Population: State Formation, Statistics, and the Census of Canada, 1840–1875*. Toronto, Ontario: University of Toronto Press.

Cyril, Malkia. 2016. "e-Carceration: Race, Technology, and the Future of Policing and Prisons in America." *Center for Media Justice*, 16 November. Available at: http://centerformediajustice.org/2016/11/16/e-carceration/ (accessed 3 January 2018).

Dai, Wenqian. 2016. "Demographic Transition." In Constance L. Shehan, ed., *The Wiley Blackwell Encyclopedia of Family Studies*, pp. 545–549. Hoboken, NJ: Wiley.

Daum, Meghan (ed.) 2016. *Selfish, Shallow and Absorbed: Sixteen Writers on the Decision Not to Have Kids*. New York: Picador/Macmillan.

Davis, Angela Y. 1981. *Women, Race and Class*. New York: Random House.

—. 2003. *Are Prisons Obsolete?* New York: Seven Stories Press.

—. 2016. *Freedom Is a Constant Struggle: Ferguson, Palestine, and the Foundations of a Movement*. Chicago, IL: Haymarket Press.

Davies, Jeremy. 2016. *The Birth of the Anthropocene*. Berkeley: University of California Press.

De la Cadena, Marisol. 2015. *Earth Beings. Ecologies of Practice Across Andean Worlds*. Durham, NC: Duke University Press.

—. 2016. "Uncommoning Nature." *E-flux Journal 56th Venice Biennale*, 22 August. Available at: http://supercommunity.e-flux.com/authors/marisol-de-la-cadena/ (accessed 18 December 2017).

Deloria, Philip. 1998. *Playing Indian*. New Haven, CT: Yale University Press.

Demos, T.J. 2016. *Decolonizing Nature: Contemporary Art and the Politics of Ecology*. Berlin: Sternberg Press.

—. 2017. *Against the Anthropocene: Visual Culture and Environment Today*. Berlin: Sternberg Press.

Denial, Catherine. 2013. *Making Marriage: Husbands, Wives and the American State in Dakota and Ojibwe Country*. St. Paul: Minnesota Historical Society Press.

Dery, Mark. 1994. "Black to the Future: Interviews with Samuel R. Delany, Greg Tate, and Tricia Rose." In Mark Dery, ed., *Flame Wars: The Discourse of Cyberculture*, pp. 179–222. Durham, NC: Duke University Press.

Despret, Vinciane. 2016. *What Would Animals Say If We Asked the Right Questions?* Minneapolis, MN: University of Minnesota Press.

Di Chiro, G. 2008. "Living Environmentalisms: Coalition Politics, Social Reproduction, and Environmental Justice." *Environmental Politics*, 17, n. 2, pp. 276–98.

Dippie, Brian W. 1982. *The Vanishing American: White Attitudes and U.S. Indian Policy*. Lawrence, KS: University of Kansas Press.

Dow, Katharine. 2016. *Making a Good Life: An Ethnography of Nature, Ethics, and Reproduction*. Princeton, NJ: Princeton University Press.

Dreifus, Claudia. 2017. "In Response to Trump, 'She Decides.'" *The New York Times*, February 21:D3.

DuBois, W.E.B. 1903. *The Souls of Black Folks*. Chicago: A.C. McClurg and Co. Available at http://xroads.virginia.edu/~hyper/dubois/ch01.html (accessed 3 January 2018).

Due, Tananarive. 1998. *My Soul to Keep*. New York: Harper Collins Publishers.

Duster, Troy. 2006. Presidential Address: "Comparative Perspectives and Competing Explanations: Taking on the Newly Configured Reductionist Challenge to Sociology." *American Sociological Review*, 71, (February), pp. 1–15.

Ebron, Paulla and Anna Tsing. 2017. "Feminism and the Anthropocene: Assessing the Field through Recent Books." Special Issue on Decolonial and Postcolonial Approaches, *Feminist Studies*, 43, n. 3, pp. 658–683.

EcoJustice. 2007. *Exposing Canada's Chemical Valley: An Investigation of Cumulative Air Pollution Emission in the Sarnia, Ontario Area*. Toronto, Ontario: EcoJustice, 2007.

Economy, Elizabeth. 2010. *The River Runs Black: The Environmental Challenge to China's Future*. Ithaca, NY: Cornell University Press.

Ehrlich, Paul R. 1968. *The Population Bomb: Population Control or Race to Oblivion?* New York: Ballantine Books, Inc.

Ehrlich, Paul R., Peter M. Kareiva, and Gretchen C. Daily. 2012. "Securing Natural Capital and Expanding Equity to Rescale Civilization." *Nature*, 7 June, pp. 68–73.

Emba, Christine. 2017. "Paul Ryan's Recipe for a Robust Economy: Have more Babies." *The Washington Post*, 15 December. Available at: https://www.washingtonpost.com/opinions/paul-ryans-recipe-for-a-robust-economy-have-more-babies/2017/12/15/dcd767b4-e1dc-11e7-89e8-edec16379010_story.html?tid=ss_mail&utm_term=.907176f81fa8 (accessed 20 December 2017).

Engels, Friedrich. 1902. *The Origin of the Family, Private Property, and the State*. Translated by Ernest Untermann. Chicago: Charles H. Kerr & Co. [1st German edition 1884].

Erten, Nifay. 2017. "Ethnography of the Unborn: Schools of Pregnancy and Turkish Reproductive Politics." Paper presented at the meetings of the Society for Social Studies of Science, Boston, 31 August.

Expanse, The. 2015. TV series. Mark Fergus and Hawk Ostby, creators. Available at: http://www.imdb.com/title/tt3230854/ (accessed 8 January 2018).

The F Word: A Foster-to-Adopt Story. 2017. PBS series, Indie lens Storycast. Season 1. Available at: https://www.thefwordseries.com/ (accessed 20 December 2017).

Faludi, Susan. 2013. "Death of a Revolutionary: Shulamith Firestone." *The New Yorker*, 15 April. Available at http://www.newyorker.com/magazine/2013/04/15/death-of-a-revolutionary (accessed 30 December 2017).

Fanon, Frantz. 1963. *The Wretched of the Earth*. Translated by Constance Farrington. New York: Grove Press.

—. 1967. *Black Skin, White Masks*. Translated by Charles Lam Markmann. New York: Grove Press.

Feminist Northern Network. 2015. "Sexual and Reproductive Justice in the North: A FemNorthNet Fact Sheet." Canadian Research Institute for the Advancement of Women. Available at: http://fnn.criaw-icref.ca/images/publications/1cad3c9f6d9b4448db42fb9f80e54862.pdf (accessed 13 January 2018).

Fincher, Leta Hong. 2014. *Leftover Women: The Resurgence of Gender Inequality in China.* London: Zed Books.

Firestone, Shulamith. 1972. *The Dialectic of Sex: The Case for Feminist Revolution,* rev. ed. New York: Bantam.

Fountain, Henry. 2017. "A Search for Reason in Nature's Chaos." *The New York Times,* Sept. 9:A1, 14.

Franke, Katherine. 2015. *Wedlocked: The Perils of Marriage Equality.* New York: NYU Press.

Franklin, Sarah. 2010. "Revisiting Reprotech: Firestone and the Question of Technology." In Mandy Merck and S. Sandford, eds., *Further Adventures of the Dialectic of Sex: Critical Essays on Shulamith Firestone,* pp. 29–60. London: Palgrave.

—. 2013. *Biological Relatives: IVF, Stem Cells and the Future of Kinship.* Durham, NC: Duke University Press.

Franklin, Sarah and Susan McKinnon. 2002. *Relative Values: Reconfiguring Kinship Studies.* Durham, NC: Duke University Press.

Friese, Carrie. 2013. *Cloning Wild Life: Zoos, Captivity, and the Future of Endangered Animals.* New York: New York University Press.

Fritsch, Kelly. 2015. "Gradations of Debility and Capacity: Biocapitalism and the Neoliberalization of Disability Relations." *Canadian Journal of Disability Studies,* 4, n. 2, pp. 12–48.

Frühstück, Sabine. 2003. *Colonizing Sex: Sexology and Social Control in Modern Japan.* Berkeley: University of California Press.

Garrett, Eilidh, Chris Galley, Nicola Shelton and Robert Woods. 2006. *Infant Mortality: A Continuing Social Problem.* Hampshire, UK: Ashgate.

Garvey, Michelle. 2011. "Global Feminist Environmental Justice." *Feminist Formations,* 23, pp. 216–23.

Gatebox. n.d. "Virtual Home Robot." Available at https://gatebox.ai/ (accessed 12 January 2018)

Georgescu, Calin. 2012. "Report of the Special Rapporteur on the Implications for Human Rights of the Environmentally Sound Management and Disposal of Hazardous Substances and Wastes." United Nations General Assembly, Human Rights Council. Available at: http://www.ohchr.org/Documents/HRBodies/HRCouncil/RegularSession/Session21/A-HRC-21-48-Add1_en.pdf (accessed 3 January 2018).

Gilbert, Scott F. 2017. "Developmental Biology: The Stem Cell of Biological Disciplines." *PLOS Biology*, 15, n. 12: e2003691. Available at: https://doi.org/10.1371/journal.pbio.2003691 (accessed 15 January 2018).

Gilbert, Scott F., Jan Sapp, and Alfred I. Tauber. 2012. "A Symbiotic View of Life: We Have Never Been Individuals." *The Quarterly Review of Biology*, 87, n. 4, pp. 325–41.

Gilbert, Scott F., Thomas C. G. Bosch, and Cristina Ledón-Rettig. 2015. "Eco-Evo-Devo: Developmental Symbiosis and Developmental Plasticity as Evolutionary Agents." *Nature Reviews Genetics*, 16, n. 10, pp. 611–22. Available at: https://doi.org/10.1038/nrg3982 (accessed 15 January 2018).

Gilbert, Scott F. and Clara Pinto-Correia. 2017. *Fear, Wonder, and Science in the New Age of Reproductive Biotechnology.* New York: Columbia University Press.

Gilmore, Ruth Wilson. 2004. "Pierce the Future for Hope: Mothers and Prisoners in the Post Keynesian California Landscape." In Julia Sudbury, ed., *Global Lockdown: Gender, Race, and the Prison Industrial Complex*, pp. 231–254. New York: Routledge.

—. 2007. *Golden Gulag: Prisons, Surplus, Crisis, and Opposition in Globalizing California.* Berkeley, CA: University of California Press.

Ginsberg, Faye and Rayna Rapp (eds.) 1995. *Conceiving the New World Order: The Global Stratification of Reproduction.* Berkeley, CA: University of California Press.

Gomez, Jewelle. 2005. *The Gilda Stories.* Ann Arbor, MI: Firebrand Books.

Government of Canada, Health Canada. 2010. "Report on Human Biomonitoring of Environmental Chemicals in Canada." Available at: http://www.hc-sc.gc.ca/ewh-semt/pubs/contaminants/chms-ecms/index-eng.php#n5_5 (accessed 13 January 2018).

Gordon, Leslie. 2017. "New Report Faults California's Electronic Monitoring of Youth." *Berkeley Law News*, 11 July. Available at: https://www.law.berkeley.edu/article/new-report-faults-californias-electronic-monitoring-youth/ (accessed 3 January 2018).

Gossett, Che. 2014. "We Will Not Rest in Peace: AIDS, Activism, Black Radicalism, Queer and/or Trans Resistance." In Jan Haritaworn, Adi Kuntsman, and Silvia Posocco, eds., *Queer Necropolitics*, pp. 31–50, New York: Routledge.

Graham, Charlotte. 2017. "Pain of Australia's 'Stolen Generation' Imbues Voice of a Celebrated Poet." *The New York Times*, Sept. 9:A6.

Greenhalgh, Susan, ed. 1995. *Situating Fertility: Anthropology and Demographic Inquiry*. Cambridge, UK: Cambridge University Press.

Greenhalgh, Susan. 1996. "The Social Construction of Population Science: An Intellectual, Institutional and Political History of 20th Century Demography." *Comparative Studies in Society and History*, 38 n. 1, pp. 26–66.

—. 2008. *Just One Child: Science and Policy in Deng's China*. Berkeley, CA: University of California Press.

—. 2009. "The Chinese Biopolitical: Facing the Twenty-first Century." *New Genetics and Society*, 28, n. 3, pp. 205–222.

Grzanka, Patrick R., Jenny Dyck Brian and Janet K. Shim. 2016. "My Bioethics Will Be Intersectional or It Will Be [Bleep]." *American Journal of Bioethics*, 16, n.4, pp. 27–29.

The Guardian. 2015. "Overpopulation, Overconsumption—in Pictures." 1 April 2015. Available at: http://www.theguardian.com/global-development-professionals-network/gallery/2015/apr/01/over-population-over-consumption-in-pictures (accessed 13 January 2018).

Guyer, Jane I. and Samuel M. Eno Belinga. 1995. "Wealth in People as Wealth in Knowledge: Accumulation and Composition in Equatorial Africa." *Journal of African History*, 36, n. 1, pp. 91-120.

Ha, Jung-ok. 2017. "Solving Low Fertility Rate with Technology." In Angela Ki Che Leung and Izumi Nakayama, eds., *Gender, Health and History in Modern East Asia*, pp. 115–135. Hong Kong: Hong Kong University Press.

Hairston, Andrea. 2016. *Will Do Magic for Small Change*. Seattle: Aqueduct Press.

Hakim, Danny. 2015. "Sex Education in Europe Turns to Urging More Births." *The New York Times*, 4 April. Available at: http://www.nytimes.com/2015/04/09/business/international/sex-education-in-europe-turns-to-urging-more-births.html?_r=0 (accessed 18 August 2016).

Halfon, Saul. 2007. *The Cairo Consensus: Demographic Surveys, Women's Empowerment, and Regime Change in Population Policy*. Lanham, MD: Rowman and Littlefield Pubs., Inc.

Hamraie, Aimi. 2017. *Building Access: Universal Design and the Politics of Disability*. Minneapolis, MN: University of Minnesota Press.

Hanssmann, Christoph. 2017. *Care in Transit: The Political and Clinical Emergence of Trans Health*. Doctoral dissertation in sociology, University of California, San Francisco.

Haraway, Donna. 1979. "The Biological Enterprise: Sex, Mind, and Profit from Human Engineering to Sociobiology." *Radical History Review*, n. 20 (Spring/Summer), pp. 206–37.

—. 1985, 2016. "A Manifesto for Cyborgs." *Socialist Review*, 80 (March-April), pp. 65-107. Reprinted in Donna Haraway, 2016, "A Cyborg Manifesto," *Manifestly Haraway*, pp. 3–90. Minneapolis, MN: University of Minnesota Press.

—. 1990. *Primate Visions: Gender, Race, and Nature in the World of Modern Science*. New York: Routledge.

—. 1991. *Simians, Cyborgs and Women: The Reinvention of Nature*. New York: Routledge.

—. 1997. "Fetus: The Virtual Speculum in the New World Order." In Donna Haraway, *Modest Witness@Second Millennium*, pp. 173-212, 299–309. New York: Routledge.

—. 1997 [2018]. *Modest_Witness@Second_Millennium. FemaleMan©_Meets_Oncomouse™*. New York: Routledge, 2nd edition with Introduction and Study Guide by Thyrza Goodeve, 2018.

—. 2010. "When Species Meet: Staying With the Trouble." *Environment and Planning D: Society and Space*, 28, n. 1, pp. 53–55.

—. 2015. "Anthropocene, Capitalocene, Plantationocene, Chthulucene: Making Kin." *Environmental Humanities*, 6, pp. 159–65.

—. 2016. *Staying with the Trouble: Making Kin in the Chthulucene*. Durham, NC: Duke University Press.

—. 2017. "Letter." *London Review of Books* 39, n. 13, 29 June. Available at: https://www.lrb.co.uk/v39/n13/letters (accessed 26 September 2017).

Haraway, Donna, Noboru Ishikawa, Scott F. Gilbert, Kenneth Olwig, Anna L. Tsing, and Nils Bubandt. 2016. "Anthropologists Are Talking–About the Anthropocene." *Journal of Anthropology*, 81, n. 3, pp. 535–64. Available at: https://doi.org/10.1080/00141844.2015.1105838 (accessed 9 January 2018).

Hardin, Garrett. 1993. *Living within the Limits: Ecology, Economics, and Population Taboos.* New York: Oxford University Press.

Harding, Susan. Forthcoming. "Religion: It's Not What It Used to Be." In Jeremy MacClancy, ed., *Exotic No More: Anthropology on the Front Lines.* Chicago, IL: University of Chicago Press, 2nd ed.

Harney, Stefano and Fred Moten. 2013. *The Undercommons: Fugitive Planning & Black Study.* London: Autonomedia/ Minor Compositions.

Harris, Cheryl. 1993. "Whiteness as Property," *Harvard Law Review*, 106, n. 8 , June, pp. 1707–1791.

Hartman, Saidiya. 1997. *Scenes of Subjection: Terrorism, Slavery, and Self-Making in the 19th Century.* Oxford, UK: Oxford University Press.

—. 2007. *Lose Your Mother: A Journey Along the Transatlantic Slave Route.* New York: Farrar, Straus and Giroux.

Hartmann, Betsy. 1987, 1995, 2016. *Reproductive Rights and Wrongs: The Global Politics of Population Control.* New York: Harper & Row, Inc., 1st ed. Boston: South End Press, 2nd ed. Chicago, IL: Haymarket Books, 3rd ed.

Harwood, Karey. 2009. "Egg Freezing: A Breakthrough for Reproductive Autonomy?" *Bioethics*, 23, n. 1, pp. 39–46.

Hawkins, Derek. 2017. "Judge to Inmates: Get Sterilized and I'll Shave Off Jail Time." *The Washington Post*, 21 July. Available at: https://www.washingtonpost.com/news/morning-mix/wp/2017/07/21/judge-to-inmates-get-sterilized-and-ill-shave-off-jail-time/?utm_term=.a2af02f044e8 (accessed 3 January 2018).

Heard, Edith, and Robert A. Martienssen. 2014. "Transgenerational Epigenetic Inheritance: Myths and Mechanisms." *Cell*, 157, n. 1, pp. 95–109.

Heise, Ursula. 2016. *Imagining Extinction: The Cultural Meanings of Endangered Species.* Chicago, IL: University of Chicago Press.

Hess, David J. 2016. *Undone Science: Social Movements, Mobilized Publics, and Industrial Transitions.* Cambridge, MA: MIT Press.

@hijinksensue, Twitter post, 12/3/2014 7:28pm. Available at: https://twitter.com/hijinksensue/status/540301586896281601 (accessed 3 January 2018).

Hodges, S. 2008. *Contraception, Colonialism and Commerce: Birth Control in South India, 1920–1940.* Burlington, VT: Ashgate Publishing Company.

Homei, Aya and Yu-Ling Huang. 2016. "Introduction: Population Control in Cold War Asia." Special issue: Population Control and Reproductive Politics in Cold War Asia. *East Asian Science, Technology, and Society: An International Journal*, 10, n. 4, pp. 343–353.

Hoover, Elizabeth, Katsi Cook, Ron Plain, Kathy Sanchez, Vi Waghiyi, Pamela Miller, Renee Dufault, Caitlin Sislin, and David O. Carpenter. 2012. "Indigenous Peoples of North America: Environmental Exposures and Reproductive Justice." *Environmental Health Perspectives*, 120, n. 12, December, pp. 1645–1649.

Hopkinson, Nalo. 1998. *Brown Girl in the Ring.* New York: Warner Books.

Hsu, A. et al. 2016. "2016 Environmental Performance Index." Yale Center for Environmental Law and Policy. Available at http://epi.yale.edu/sites/default/files/2016EPI_Full_Report_opt.pdf (accessed 1 January 2018).

Huang, Yu-ling. 2016. "Bio-political Knowledge in the Making: Population Politics and Fertility Studies in Early Cold War Taiwan." *East Asian Science, Technology and Society: An International Journal*, 10, n. 4, pp. 377–399.

@hunktears, Twitter post, 12/3/2014, 9:54pm. Available at https://twitter.com/hunktears/status/540338424587091968 (accessed 3 January 2018)

Hutchinson, G. Evelyn. 1978. *An Introduction to Population Ecology.* New Haven, CT: Yale University Press.

Imarisha, Walida and Adrienne Maree Brown. 2015. *Octavia's Brood: Science Fiction Stories from Social Justice Movements.* Oakland, CA: AK Press.

Inhorn, Marcia C. and Pasquale Patrizio. 2015. "Infertility Around the Globe: New Thinking on Gender, Reproductive Technologies and Global Movements in the 21st Century." *Human Reproduction Update*, 21, n. 4, pp. 411–426.

Inter-Faith Council for Social Service. 2017. "Support Circles." Available at: http://www.unhcr.org/en-us/figures-at-a-glance.html (accessed 20 December 2017).

International Geosphere-Biosphere Program. 2015. "Great Acceleration - IGBP." Available at: http://www.igbp.net/globalchange/greatacceleration.4.1b8ae20512db692f2a680001630.html (accessed 13 January 2018).

@Its____abby, Twitter post, 12/5/2014, 5:59pm. Available at: https://twitter.com/its____abby/status/541004068651814913 (accessed 3 January 2018).

The Japan Times. 2016. "Chiba Municipality to Offer Young Women Subsidies to Freeze Their Eggs." 10 June. Available at: https://www.japantimes.co.jp/news/2016/06/10/national/science-health/chiba-hospital-conducts-first-local-government-subsidized-egg-freezing/#.WcnnghOCyV4 (accessed 1 January 2018).

Jemison, N.K. 2010. *The Hundred Thousand Kingdoms*. New York: Orbit Books.

Jervis, Coco. 2015. "The Great LARC Debate: Facilitating a Balanced Approach to Education and Promotion of LARCs." *The Women's Health Activist*, July-August, pp. 4–5. Washington, D.C.: National Women's Health Network.

Johnson, Corey G. 2013. "Female Inmates Sterilized in California Prisons Without Approval," 7 July. *Reveal: The Center for Investigative Reporting*. Available at: https://www.revealnews.org/article/female-inmates-sterilized-in-california-prisons-without-approval/ (accessed 3 January 2018).

Johnson, Walter. 2015. "Ferguson's Fortune 500 Company." *The Atlantic*, 26 April. Available at: https://www.theatlantic.com/politics/archive/2015/04/fergusons-fortune-500-company/390492/ (accessed 3 January 2018).

Jones, Gavin, Paulin Tay Straughan, and Angelique Chan, eds. 2009. *Ultra-low Fertility in Pacific Asia: Trends, Causes and Policy Issues*. London, UK: Routledge.

Joseph, Miranda. 2002. *Against the Romance of Community*. Minneapolis, MN: University of Minnesota Press.

Kaba, Mariame. 2017. "Help Criminalized Survivors of Violence For the Holidays!" *Prison Culture*, 15 November. Available at: http://www.usprisonculture.com/blog/2017/11/15/help-criminalized-survivors-of-violence-for-the-holidays/ (accessed 3 January 2018).

Kabasenche, William P., and Michael K. Skinner. 2014. "DDT, Epigenetic Harm, and Transgenerational Environmental Justice." *Environmental Health*, 13, n. 1, p. 62. Available at: https://doi.org/10.1186/1476-069X-13-62 (accessed 15 January 2018).

Kimmerer, Robin Wall. 2015. "Nature Needs a New Pronoun: To Stop the Age of Extinction, Let's Start by Ditching 'It'." *Yes Magazine*, 30 March. Available at: http://www.yesmagazine.org/issues/together-with-earth/alternative-grammar-a-new-language-of-kinship (accessed 18 August 2016).

King, Helen H. 1970. "It's Easier to Adopt Today," *Ebony*, 26, n. 2, pp. 120–128.

Kingsland, Sharon. 1985. *Modeling Nature: Episodes in the History of Population Ecology*. Chicago, IL: University of Chicago Press.

Kirksey, Eben, ed. 2014. *The Multispecies Salon*. Durham, NC: Duke University Press.

Koide, Jamie. 2016. "Singaporeans are Getting Creative When it Comes to Combating the Low Fertility Rate." *SoraNews* 24, 5 February. Available at https://en.rocketnews24.com/2016/02/05/singaporeans-are-getting-creative-when-it-comes-to-combating-the-low-fertility-rate/ (accessed 12 January 2018).

Kolbert, Elizabeth. 2014. *The Sixth Extinction: An Unnatural History*. New York: Henry Holt.

Krause, E. L. and M. Marchesi. 2007. "Fertility Politics as 'Social Viagra': Reproducing Boundaries, Social Cohesion, and Modernity in Italy." *American Anthropologist*, 109, n. 2, pp. 350–62.

Krolokke, Charlotte, Lene Myong, Stine W. Adrian and Tine Tjornhoj-Thomsen. 2016. *Critical Kinship Studies*. London and New York: Rowman and Littlefield, International.

Kuletz, Valerie. 1998. *Tainted Desert: Environmental and Social Ruin in the American West*. New York: Routledge.

Kunkel, Benjamin. 2017. "The Capitalocene." *London Review of Books*, 2 March, pp. 22-28.

Kunuk, Zacharias and Ian Mauro. 2010. *Inuit Knowledge and Climate Change*. IsumaTV, Isuma Distribution International. Available at: http://www.isuma.tv/inuit-knowledge-and-climate-change (accessed 18 August 2016).

LaDuke, Winona. 2017. "Cultivating Resistance and Lighting the Eighth Fire: Challenging the Fossil Fuel Industry and Restoring Anishinaabe Economics." Presented at the conference "Water is Life, But Many Can't Drink It," University of Toronto, 24 September.

Landler, Mark. 2017. "President Again Says Both Sides Share Blame in Charlottesville." *The New York Times*, September 15:A15.

Langston, Nancy. 2010. *Toxic Bodies: Hormone Disruptors and the Legacy of DES*. New Haven, CT: Yale University Press.

Latour, Bruno. 1999. "On Recalling ANT." *Sociological Review*, 47, n. S1, pp.15–25.

Lee, Jaeah. 2016. "Cleveland Asked Tamir Rice's Family to Pay $500 for Their Child's Last Ambulance Ride." *Mother Jones*, 11 February. Available at: http://www.motherjones.com/politics/2016/02/cleveland-tamir-rice-family-pay-ambulance/ (accessed 3 January 2018).

Lee, Ronald and Andrew Mason. 2006. "Back to Basics: What is Demographic Dividend?" *Finance and Development*, 43, n. 3, pp. 16–17.

Lee, Ronald, Andrew Mason, and members of the NTA Network. 2014. "Is Low Fertility Really a Problem? Population Aging, Dependency, and Consumption." *Science*, 346, n. 6206, pp. 229–234.

Lewis, Simon and Mark Maslin. 2015. "Defining the Anthropocene." *Nature*, 518, pp. 171–189.

Lewis, Sophie. 2017. "Cthulhu Plays No Role for Me." *Viewpoint Magazine*, 8 May. Available at: https://www.viewpointmag.com/2017/05/08/cthulhu-plays-no-role-for-me/ (accessed 26 September 2017).

Living Blue Planet Report. 2015. Available at: http://www.livingplanetindex.org/projects?main_page_project=BluePlanetReport&home_flag=1 (accessed 4 August 2016).

Lorenzo, Rachael. 2016. "At Standing Rock, Environmental Justice Is Reproductive Justice." September 20. Available at: https://rewire.news/article/2016/09/20/standing-rock-environmental-justice-reproductive-justice/ (accessed 9 January 2018).

Ludden, Jennifer. 2016. "Should We Be Having Kids in the Age of Climate Change?" Aired on "All Things Considered," *National Public Radio*, August 18. Available at: http://www.npr.org/2016/08/18/479349760/should-we-be-having-kids-in-the-age-of-climate-change (accessed 1 January 2018).

Lutz, Wolfgang, William P. Butz, and K.C. Samir. 2014. *World Population & Human Capital in the Twenty-First Century*. Oxford, UK: Oxford University Press.

Lyons, Kristina. 2016. "Decomposition as Life Politics: Soil, Selva, and Small Farmers under the Gun of the U.S.-Columbia War on Drugs." *Cultural Anthropology*, 31, n. 1, pp. 56–81. Available at: https://culanth.org/articles/800-decomposition-as-life-politics-soils (accessed 18 August 2016).

Ma, Julie. 2014. "25 Famous Women on Childlessness." *New York Magazine*, September 15. Available at https://www.thecut.com/2014/08/25-famous-women-on-childlessness.html (accessed 1 January 2018).

Mackinnon, Alison. 1995. "Were Women Present at the Demographic Transition? Questions from a Feminist Historian to Historical Demographers." *Gender and History*, 7, n. 2, pp. 222–40.

Maheswari, Sapna and Alexandra Stevenson. 2017. "Major Sites Face Rebuke for Ads Tied to Racism." *The New York Times*, 16 September 16:A1, B4.

Malm, Andreas. 2016. *Fossil Capital: The Rise of Steam Power and the Roots of Global Warming*. London, UK: Verso Books.

Masco, Joseph. 2010. "Bad Weather: On Planetary Crisis." *Social Studies of Science*, 40, n. 1, pp. 7–40.

Maternowska, M. C. 2006. *Reproducing Inequities: Poverty and the Politics of Population in Haiti*. New Brunswick, NJ: Rutgers University Press.

McCann, Carole R. 2016. *Figuring the Population Bomb: Gender and Demography in the Mid-Twentieth Century*. Seattle, WA: University of Washington Press.

McClain, Dani. 2014. "The Murder of Black Youth Is a Reproductive Justice Issue." *The Nation*, 13 August. Available at: https://www.thenation.com/article/murder-black-youth-reproductive-justice-issue/ (accessed 15 January 2018).

M'charek, Amade. 2013. "Beyond Fact or Fiction: On the Materiality of Race in Practice." *Cultural Anthropology*, 28, n.3, pp. 420–442.

McKittrick, Katherine. 2013. "Plantation Futures." *Small Axe: A Caribbean Journal of Criticism*, 17, n. 3 (42), pp. 1–15. Available at: https://doi.org/10.1215/07990537-2378892 (accessed 15 January 2018).

McKittrick, Katherine, ed. 2015. *Sylvia Wynter: On Being Human as Praxis.* Durham, NC: Duke University Press Books.

Mehta, Lyla. 2016. "Diane Rocheleau: The Feminist Political Ecology Legacy and Beyond." In W. Harcourt, ed., *The Palgrave Handbook of Gender and Development*, pp. 262–75. Zurich: Springer.

Mennonite Central Committee. 2017. "Refugee Response." Available at: https://mcccanada.ca/learn/what/refugees/sponsorship (accessed 20 September 2017).

Meyerson, Collier. 2016. "Read the Short, Devastating Speech Sandra Bland's Mother Just Made to Congressional Leaders." *Splinter*, 28 April. Available at: https://splinternews.com/read-the-short-devastating-speech-sandra-blands-mother-1793856494 (accessed 3 January 2018).

Michaelson, Karen L. 1981. *And the Poor Get Children: Radical Perspectives on Population Dynamics.* New York: Monthly Review Press.

Minton, Todd D. and Zhen Zheng. 2015. "Jail Inmates at Midyear 2014." *U.S. Department of Justice*. Available at: https://www.bjs.gov/content/pub/pdf/jim14.pdf (accessed 3 January 2018).

Mitchell, Audra and Zoe Todd. 2016. "Earth Violence: Indigeneity and the Anthropocene." Lecture at University of Wisconsin Milwaukee, 6 May. Available at: https://worldlyir.files.wordpress.com/2016/04/earth-violence-text-mitchell-and-todd.pdf (accessed 18 December 2017).

Mitman, Gregg. 2016. "Life in the Ruins." Books Forum. *BioSocieties*, 11, n. 3, pp. 396–400.

Mol, Anemarie. 2008. *The Logic of Care: Health and the Problem of Patient Choice.* London: Routledge.

Moon, Seungsook. 2005. *Militarized Modernity and Gendered Citizenship in South Korea*. Durham, NC: Duke University Press.

Moore, Jason. 2015. *Capitalism in the Web of Life: Ecology and the Accumulation of Capital*. London, UK: Verso.

Moore, Jason, ed. 2016. *Anthropocene or Capitalocene? Nature, History, and the Crisis of Capitalism*. Oakland, CA: PM Press.

Moreton-Robinson, Aileen. 2015. *The White Possessive: Property, Power, and Indigenous Sovereignty*. Minneapolis and London: University of Minnesota Press.

Morgensen, Scott Lauria. 2011. *Spaces Between Us: Queer Settler Colonialism and Indigenous Decolonization*. Minneapolis, MN: University of Minnesota Press.

Morrison, Toni. 1987. *Beloved*. New York: Vintage International.

Mortimer-Sandilands, Catriona and Bruce Erickson. 2010. *Queer Ecologies: Sex, Nature, Politics, Desire*. Bloomington, IN: Indiana University Press.

Mount, Ferdinand. 2017. "Umbrageousness." *London Review of Books*, 7 September, pp. 3, 6–8.

Murphey, David and P. Mae Cooper. 2015. "Parents Behind Bars: What Happens to the Children?" *October*. Available at: http://www.childtrends.org/wp-content/uploads/2015/10/2015-42ParentsBehindBars.pdf (accessed 3 January 2018).

Murphy, Michelle. 2006. *Sick Building Syndrome and the Problem of Uncertainty: Environmental Politics, Technoscience, and Women Workers*. Durham, NC: Duke University Press.

—. 2011. "Distributed Reproduction." In Monica Casper and Paisley Currah, eds., *Corpus: An Interdisciplinary Reader on Bodies and Knowledge*, pp.21–28. New York: Palgrave.

—. 2012. *Seizing the Means of Reproduction: Entanglements of Feminism, Health, and Technoscience*. Durham, NC: Duke University Press.

—. 2013. "Economization of Life." In Peg Rawes, ed., *Relational Architectural Ecologies: Architecture, Nature and Subjectivity*, pp. 139–155. London, UK: Oxford University Press.

—. 2015. "Unsettling Care: Troubling Transnational Itineraries of Care in Feminist Health Practices." *Social Studies of Science*, 45, n. 5, pp. 717–737.

—. 2016. *The Economization of Life*. Durham, NC: Duke University Press.

Mutler, Allison, Gillian Wong and David Crary. 2017. "Global Effort to Get Kids Out of Orphanages Advancing." *San Francisco Chronicle*, 20 December, A4.

National Transfer Accounts Project. n.d. "National Transfer Accounts: Understanding the Generational Economy." Available at http://www.ntaccounts.org/web/nta/show (accessed 12 January 2018).

National Women's Health Network. n.d. "National Women's Health Network Website." Available at: https://www.nwhn.org/ (accessed 10 January 2018).

Native American Women's Health Education Resource Center. n.d. "Reproductive Justice Program." Available at: http://www.nativeshop.org/programs/reproductive-justice.html (accessed 20 December 2017).

Native Youth Sexual Health Network. n.d. "Environmental Violence and Reproductive Justice." Available at: http://www.nativeyouthsexualhealth.com/ environmentalviolenceandreproductivejustice.html (accessed 15 January 2018).

Native Youth Sexual Health Network and Women's Earth Alliance. 2016. "Violence on the Land, Violence on Our Bodies: Building an Indigenous Response to Environmental Violence." Available at: http://landbodydefense.org/uploads/files/ VLVBReportToolkit2016.pdf (accessed 15 January 2018).

Nelson, Alondra. 2008. "Bio Science: Genetic Genealogy Testing and the Pursuit of African American Ancestry." *Social Studies of Science*, 38, n. 5, pp. 759–783.

—. 2013. *Body and Soul: The Black Panther Party and the Fight against Medical Discrimination*. Minneapolis, MN: University of Minnesota Press.

—. 2016. *The Social Life of DNA: Race, Reparations, and Reconciliation After the Genome*. Boston, MA: Beacon Press.

Nelson, Diane M. 2015. *Who Counts? The Mathematics of Death and Life after Genocide*. Durham, NC: Duke University Press.

Nelson, Jennifer. 2003. *Women of Color and the Reproductive Rights Movement*. New York: New York University Press.

Newman, Amie. 2017. "The Status of Black Women in the United States." *Our Bodies, Our Selves*, 19 June. Available at: https://www.ourbodiesourselves.org/2017/06/a-new-report-the-status-of-black-women-in-the-united-states/ (accessed 9 January 2018).

The New York Times. 2017. "The President's Words on Hatred and History." *The New York Times*, 16 August, A12.

NHK. 2010. "無縁社会." ["Society without Connections: A Documentary"]. Tokyo: NHK Muen Shkai Project Shuzia-han. (In Japanese: NHK. 2010. Muen Shakai Documentary. Tokyo: NHK Muen Shkai Project Shuzia-han.)

Ochiai, Emiko. 2014. "Leaving the West, Rejoining the East? Gender and Family in Japan's Semi-Compressed Modernity." *International Sociology*, 29, n.3, pp. 209–228.

O'Connor, Kevin, Duskin Drum, and Paulette Metuq. 2017. "Wear Qisi-Become Seal." *Performance Research*, 22, n. 2, pp. 20–26.

@Official_Lov, Twitter post, 12/3/2014, 6:48pm. Available at: https://twitter.com/Official_Lov/status/ 540291640951590912 (accessed 3 January 2018).

Okorafor, Nnedi. 2015. *Binti*. New York: Tor Books.

Olszynko-Gryn, Jesse. 2014. "Laparoscopy as a Technology of Population Control." In Heinrich Hartmann and Corinna R. Unger, eds., *A World of Populations: Transnational Perspectives on Demography in the Twentieth Century*, pp. 147–177. New York: Bergham.

O'Neil, B C, Brant Liddle, Leiwen Jiang, Kirk R. Smith, Shonali Pachauri, Michael Dalton and Regina Fuchs. 2012. "Demographic Change and Carbon Dioxide Emissions" *Lancet*, 380, n. 9837, pp. 157–164.

O'Riordon, Kate and Joan Haran. 2009. "From Reproduction to Research: Sourcing Eggs, IVF and Cloning in the UK." *Feminist Theory*, 10, n. 2, pp. 191–210.

Ostrander, Madeline. 2016. "How Do You Decide to Have a Baby When Climate Change is Remaking Life on Earth?" *The Nation*, 11–18 April: Available at: https://www.thenation.com/article/how-do-you-decide-to-have-a-baby-when-climate-change-is-remaking-life-on-earth/ (accessed 1 January 2018).

Oudshoorn, Nelly. 1996. "The Decline of the One-size-fits-all Paradigm, or How Reproductive Scientists Try to Cope with Postmodernity." In Nina Lykke and Rosi Braidotti, eds., *Between Monsters, Goddesses, and Cyborgs: Feminist Confrontations with Science, Medicine, and Cyberspace*, pp. 153–173. London, UK: ZED Books.

—. 2003. *The Male Pill: A Biography of a Technology in the Making*. Durham, NC: Duke University Press.

Oxfam Media Briefing. 2015, December 2. "Extreme Carbon Inequality." Available at: https://www.oxfam.org/en/research/extreme-carbon-inequality (accessed 18 December 2017).

Paik, Young-Gyung. 2014. "Assisted Reproductive Technologies at Crossroads: Neoliberal Economy, National Depopulation Crisis, and the Politics of Reproduction in South Korea." In Sarojini N and Vrinda Marwah, eds., *Reconfiguring Reproduction: Feminist Health Perspectives on Assisted Reproductive Technologies*. New Delhi: Zubaan Books.

Palmer, Brian. 2017. "For the Forgotten African American Dead," *The New York Times*, 7 January. Available at: https://www.nytimes.com/2017/01/07/opinion/sunday/for-the-forgotten-african-american-dead.html (accessed 8 January 2018).

Peck, Ellen and Judith Senderowitz (eds.) 1974. *Pronatalism: The Myth of Mom and Apple Pie*. New York: Thomas Y. Crowell Company.

Peck, Raoul, director. 2017. *I Am Not Your Negro*. Documentary film. Production Company: Velvet Film.

Perdue, Theda. 1980. *Nations Remembered: An Oral History of the Five Civilized Tribes, 1865–1907*. Westport, CN: Greenwood Press.

Pet Food Industry. 2017. Available at: https://www.petfoodindustry.com/ (accessed 21 December 2017).

Petchesky, Rosalind P. and Karen Judd, eds. 1998. *Negotiating Reproductive Rights: Women's Perspectives Across Countries and Cultures*. London, UK: Zed Books.

Philipps, Dave. 2017. "Top Leaders of Military Condemn Hate Groups." *The New York Times*, August 17, A16.

Pickens, Josie. 2016. "#FlintWaterCrisis Is a Reproductive Justice Issue." *Ebony*, 2 February. Available at: http://www.ebony.com/news-views/flint-water-crisis-reproductive-justice (accessed 15 January 2018).

Pignarre, Philippe and Isabelle Stengers. 2005. *La Sorcellerie Capitaliste: Pratiques de Désenvoutement*. Paris: Éditions de la Decouverte.

Plumwood, Val. 1993. *Feminism and the Mastery of Nature*. London, UK: Routledge.

Pollitt, Katha. 2015. "Reclaiming Abortion Rights." *Dissent*, Fall. Available at: https://www.dissentmagazine.org/article/reclaiming-abortion-rights-katha-pollitt (accessed 1 January 2018).

Pollock, Anne. 2015. "On the Suspended Sentences of the Scott Sisters: Mass Incarceration, Kidney Donation, and the Biopolitics of Race in the United States." *Science, Technology, & Human Values*, 40, n. 2, pp. 250–271.

Ponte-Toyama. n.d. "Café." Available at: https://ponte-toyama.com/cafe/ (accessed 12 January 2018).

Population and Development Program. n.d. "PopDev/Hampshire College." Available at: http://popdev.hampshire.edu (accessed 10 January 2018).

Population Matters. 2018. "Population Matters: For a Sustainable Future." Available at: https://www.populationmatters.org/about/overview/ (accessed 6 January 2018).

Puig de la Bellacasa, Maria. 2011. "Matters of Care in Technoscience: Assembling Neglected Things." *Social Studies of Science*, 41, n. 1, pp. 85–106.

Puig, Maria de la Bellacasa. 2015. "Making Time for Soil: Technoscientific Futurity and the Pace of Care." *Social Studies of Science*, 45, n. 5, pp. 691–716.

Rahman, Mohammad Mafizur. 2017. "Do Population Density, Economic Growth, Energy Use and Experts Adversely Affect Environmental Quality in Asian Populous Countries?" *Renewable and Sustainable Energy Review*, 77, September, pp. 506–514. Available at: http://www.sciencedirect.com/science/article/pii/S1364032117305427 (accessed 15 January 2018).

Rambukkana, Nathan. 2015. *Fraught Intimacies: Non/Monogamy in the Public Sphere*. Vancouver and Toronto: UBC Press.

Ramzy, Austin. 2016. "Taiwan Apologizes to Aborigines for Injustices." *The New York Times*, 2 August, A9.

Rapping, Elayne. 1990. "The Future of Motherhood: Some Unfashionably Visionary Thoughts." In Karen V. Hansen and Ilene J. Philipson, eds., *Women, Class, and the Feminist Imagination: A Socialist Feminist Reader*, pp. 537–548. Philadelphia, PA: Temple University Press.

Raymo, James, Hyunjoon Park, Yu Xie, and Wei-jun Jean Yeung. 2015. "Marriages and Family in East Asia: Continuity and Change." *Annual Review of Sociology*, 41, pp. 471–492.

Reardon, Jenny. 2005. *Race to the Finish: Identity and Governance in an Age of Genomics*. Princeton, NJ: Princeton University Press.

—. 2017. *The Postgenomic Condition: Ethics, Justice, and Knowledge after the Genome*. Chicago, IL: University of Chicago Press.

Reproductive Sociology Research Group. n.d. "ReproSoc: Reproductive Sociology Research Group." Cambridge University. Available at: http://www.reprosoc.sociology.cam.ac.uk/ (accessed 6 January 2018).

Rich, Motoko. 2018. "Push to End South Korea Abortion Ban Gains Strength, and Signatures." *The New York Times*, 14 January, 12.

Richie, Beth. 1999. "The Social Construction of the Immoral Black Mother: Social Policy, Community Policing, and Their Effects on Youth Violence." In Adele E. Clarke and Virginia L. Olesen, eds., *Revisioning Women, Health, and Healing: Feminist, Cultural and Technoscience Perspectives*, pp. 282–302. New York: Routledge.

—. 2012. *Arrested Justice: Black Women, Violence, and America's Prison Nation*. New York: New York University Press.

Riley, Nancy. 2003. *Demography in the Age of the Postmodern*. Cambridge, UK: Cambridge University Press.

—. 2017. *Population in China*. Cambridge, UK: Polity.

Riley, Nancy and Krista E. Van Vleet. 2012. *Making Families through Adoption*. Thousand Oaks, CA: Sage.

Ripple, William J., C. Wolf, T.M. Newsome, M. Galetti, M. Alamgir, E. Crist, M. Mahmoud, W.F. Laurance, and 15,364 scientist signatories from 184 countries. 2017. "World Scientists' Warning to Humanity: A Second Notice." *BioScience*, 67, n. 12, 1 December, pp. 1026–1028. Available at: https://academic.oup.com/bioscience/article/67/12/1026/4605229 (accessed 15 January 2018).

Ritvo, Harriet. 1987. *The Animal Estate*. Cambridge, MA: Harvard University Press.

—. 1997. *The Platypus and the Mermaid and Other Figments of the Classifying Imagination*. Cambridge, MA: Harvard University Press.

Roberts, David. 2017. "The Best Way to Reduce Your Personal Carbon Emissions: Don't Be Rich." *Vox*, 14 July. Available at: https://www.vox.com/energy-and-environment/2017/7/14/15963544/climate-change-individual-choices (accessed 25 September 2017).

Roberts, Dorothy. 1997. *Killing the Black Body: Race, Reproduction, and the Meaning of Liberty*. New York: Pantheon.

—. 2002. *Shattered Bonds: The Color of Child Welfare*. New York: Civitas Books.

—. 2015. "Reproductive Justice, Not Just Rights." *Dissent* (Fall). Available at: https://www.dissentmagazine.org/article/reproductive-justice-not-just-rights (accessed 1 January 2018).

Robinson, Kim Stanley. 2012. *2312*. Boston, MA: Orbit Books.

Robinson, Tasha. 2016. "How SyFy's *The Expanse* Cast Its Multiracial Future," *The Verge*, 25 February. Available at: http://www.theverge.com/2016/2/25/11103434/syfy-the-expanse-series-diverse-cast (accessed 8 January 2018).

Rocheleau, Diane, Barbara Thomas-Slayer, and Ester Wangari, eds. 1996. *Feminist Political Ecology: Global Issues and Local Experiences*. London, UK: Routledge.

Rojas-Cheatham, Ann, Dana Ginn Parades, Shana Griffin, Aparna Shah, and Eveline Shen. 2009. "Looking Both Ways: Women's Lives at the Crossroads of Reproductive Justice and Climate Justice." In Asian Communities for Reproductive Justice, *The Momentum Series*, 5. Available at: https://forwardtogether.org/tools/looking-both-ways/ (accessed 15 January 2018).

Rose, Deborah Bird. 2006. "What If the Angel of History Were a Dog?" *Cultural Studies Review*, 12, n. 1, pp. 67–78.

Ross, Loretta. 2011. "What Is Reproductive Justice?" SisterSong Women of Color Reproductive Justice Collective. Available at: https://www.trustblackwomen.org/our-work/what-is-reproductive-justice/9-what-is-reproductive-justice (accessed 1 January 2018)

Ross, Loretta, and Rickie Solinger. 2017. *Reproductive Justice: An Introduction*. Berkeley, CA: University of California Press.

Rutherford, Charlotte. 1992. "Reproductive Freedom and African American Women." *Yale Journal of Law and Feminism*, 4, n. 2, pp. 255–90.

Saetnan, Ann, Nelly Oudshoorn, and Marta Kirejczyk, eds. 2000. *Bodies of Technology: Women's Involvement with Reproductive Medicine.* Columbus, OH: Ohio State University Press.

Sahlins, Marshall. 2013. *What Kinship Is–And Is Not.* Chicago, IL: University of Chicago Press.

Sances, Michael W. and Hye Young You. 2017. "Who Pays for Government? Descriptive Representation and Exploitative Revenue Sources." *The Journal of Politics*, 79, n. 3, pp. 1090–1094.

Santa Cruz Museum of Art and History. 2017. "Lost Childhoods: Voices of Santa Cruz County Foster Youth and the Foster Youth Museum, July 7–December 31, 2017." Available at: https://santacruzmah.org/2016/lost-childhoods-july-7-2017-december-31-2017/ (accessed 20 December 2017).

Sarkisian, Natalia and Naomi Gerstel. 2016. "Does Singlehood Isolate or Integrate? Examining the Link between Marital Status and Ties to Kin, Friends, and Neighbors." *Journal of Social and Personal Relationships*, 33, n. 3, pp. 361–384.

Sasser, Jade S. 2014a. "The Wave of the Future? Youth Advocacy at the Nexus of Population and Climate Change." *The Geographical Journal*, 180, n. 2, pp. 102–110.

—. 2014b. "From Darkness into Light: Race, Population and Environmental Advocacy." *Antipode*, 46, n. 5, pp. 1240–1257.

—. 2014c. "Giving What to Whom? Thoughts on Feminist Knowledge Production." *Journal of Research Practice*, 10, n. 2: Article N13. Available at: http://jrp.icaap.org/index.php/jrp/article/view/410/396 (accessed 9 January 2018).

Scheper-Hughes, Nancy. 1993. *Death without Weeping: The Violence of Everyday Life in Brazil.* Berkeley, CA: University of California Press.

Schoen, Johanna. 2005. *Choice and Coercion: Birth Control, Sterilization and Abortion in Public Health and Welfare.* Chapel Hill, NC: University of North Carolina Press.

Schubiner, Lindsay. 2017. "Dangerous Environmentalisms Exposed in the Era of Trump." *Different Takes*, 91 (Fall). Available at: https://sites.hampshire.edu/popdev/ (accessed 29 December 2017)

Schultz, Susanne and Daniel Bendix. 2015. "A Revival of Explicit Population Policy in Development Cooperation: The German Government, Bayer and the Gates Foundation." *Different Takes*, 89 (Fall). Population and Development Program, Hampshire College. Available at: https://sites.hampshire.edu/popdev/different-takes/ (accessed 9 January 2018).

Schwartz, Rafi. 2017. "Tennessee Inmates are Being Offered a Horrifying Choice: Jail Time or Sterilization." *Splinternews*, 20 July: Available at: https://splinternews.com/tennessee-inmates-are-being-offered-a-horrifying-choice-1797100263 (accessed 29 December 2017).

@SeanMcElwee, Twitter post, 12/4/2014, 12:05am. Available at: https://twitter.com/SeanMcElwee/status/540371368395964417 (accessed 3 January 2018).

Sebring, Sabrina. n.d. "Mississippi Appendectomy." Available at: https://mississippiappendectomy.wordpress.com (accessed 3 January 2018).

Sellers, Patricia. 2015. "Human and Ecological Health in Asubpeeschoseewagong Netum Anishinabeck (Grassy Narrows First Nation)." ANA-Ontario Mercury Working Group. Available at: http://freegrassy.net/wp-content/uploads/2015/06/ANA-Ontario-MWG-Sellers-Final-Report-2014-highlited.pdf (accessed 15 January 2018).

Sengupta, Somini and Rick Gladstone. 2017. "U.S. Cuts Off U.N. Agency That Supports Contraception." *The New York Times*, April 4, A6.

Shawl, Nisi. 2017. *Everfair: A Novel*. New York: Tor Books.

She Decides Initiative, n.d. Available at: https://www.government.nl/topics/she-decides/she-decides-initiative (accessed 6 January 2018).

Sheoran, Nayantara, Daisy Deomampo and Cecilia Van Hollen. 2015. "Extending Theory, Rupturing Boundaries: Reproduction, Health, and Medicine Beyond North–South Binaries." *Medical Anthropology*, 34, n. 3, pp. 185–191.

Shim, Janet K. 2010. "Cultural Health Capital: A Theoretical Approach to Understanding Health Care interactions and the Dynamics of Unequal Treatment." *Journal of Health and Social Behavior*, 51, no. 1, pp. 1–15.

Shorter, David Delgado. 2015. "Sexuality." In Robert Warrior, ed., *The World of Indigenous North America*, pp. 487–505. New York and London: Routledge.

—. 2016. "Spirituality." In Fred E. Hoxie, ed., *The Oxford Handbook of American Indian History*, pp. 433–57. Oxford, UK: Oxford University Press.

Shorto, Russell. 2008. "No hay bebes? Keine kinder? Nessun bambino? No babies?" *The New York Times Magazine*, 29 June, pp. 34–41, 68–71.

Shukin, Nicole. 2009. *Animal Capital: Rendering Life in Biopolitical Times*. Minneapolis, MN: University of Minnesota Press.

Silliman, Jael, Marlene G. Fried, Loretta Ross and Elena R. Gutierrez. 2004, 2016. *Undivided Rights: Women of Color Organizing for Reproductive Justice*. Cambridge, MA: South End Press, 1st ed. Chicago: Haymarket Books, 2nd ed.

Silliman, Jael and Ynestra King, eds. 1999. *Dangerous Intersections: Feminist Perspectives on Population, Environment and Development*. Cambridge, MA: South End Press.

Simone, AbdulMaliq. 2004. *For the City Yet to Come*. Durham, NC: Duke University Press.

SisterSong Women of Color Reproductive Health Collective. 2007. *Reproductive Justice Briefing Book*. Atlanta, GA: Sister Song.

SisterSong Women of Color Reproductive Health Collective. N.d. "SisterSong Women of Color Reproductive Justice Website." Available at: http://sistersong.net/ (accessed 6 January 2018).

SisterSong Women of Color Reproductive Health Collective. n.d. "What Is Reproductive Justice?" Available at: http://sistersong.net/reproductive-justice/ (accessed 1 January 2018).

Skinner, Michael K., Mohan Manikkam, Rebecca Tracey, Carlos Guerrero-Bosagna, Muksitul Haque, and Eric E Nilsson. 2013. "Ancestral Dichlorodiphenyltrichloroethane (DDT) Exposure Promotes Epigenetic Transgenerational Inheritance of Obesity." *BMC Medicine*, 11 (October), p. 228.

Skinner, Michael K., Carlos Guerrero-Bosagna and M. Muksitul Haque. 2015. "Environmentally Induced Epigenetic Transgenerational Inheritance of Sperm Epimutations Promote Genetic Mutations." *Epigenetics*, 10, n. 8, pp. 762–71. Available at: https://doi.org/10.1080/15592294.2015.1062207 (accessed 15 January 2018).

Small, Ernest. 2011. "The New Noah's Ark: Beautiful and Useful Species Only. Part 1. Biodiversity Priorities." *Biodiversity*, 12, n. 4, pp. 232–47.

Smith, Andrea. 2005. *Conquest: Sexual Violence and American Indian Genocide*. Boston, MA: South End Press.

Smith, Karl. 2012. "From Dividual and Individual Selves to Porous Subjects." *The Australian Journal of Anthropology*, 23, pp. 50–64. Available at: doi:10.1111/j.1757-6547.2012.00167.x (accessed 15 January 2018).

Smith, Martyn T., Rosemarie de la Rosa, and Sarah I. Daniels. 2015. "Using Exposomics to Assess Cumulative Risks and Promote Health." *Environmental and Molecular Mutagenesis*, 56, n. 9, pp. 715–23. Available at: http://onlinelibrary.wiley.com/doi/10.1002/em.21985/abstract;jsessionid=376D4594929ABEF901EEECF975A27826.f04t01 (accessed 15 January 2018).

Smith, Mitch. 2017. "Once Home to Masses, A Standing Rock Camp is Emptied and Razed." *The New York Times*, 24 February, A22.

Smith, Mitch and Alan Blinder. 2017. "10 Arrested in North Dakota as Pipeline Protest Camp Empties." *The New York Times*, 23 February, A12.

Solinger, Rickie and Mie Nakachi. 2016. *Reproductive States: Global Perspectives on the Invention and Implementation of Population Policy*. Oxford UK: Oxford University Press.

Spar, Debora L. 2006. *The Baby Business: How Money, Science, and Politics Drive the Commerce of Conception*. Cambridge, MA: Harvard Business School Press.

Spies Jejser (Spies Travel). 2015. "Do It for Mom" (Do It for Denmark 2). 29 September. Available at: https://www.youtube.com/watch?v=B00grl3K01g&feature=youtu.be (accessed 10 January 2018).

Spillers, Hortense. 1984, 2003. "Interstices: A Small Drama of Words." In Carole S. Vance, ed., *Pleasure and Danger: Exploring Female Sexuality*, pp. 73–100. Boston: Routledge and Kegan Paul. Reprinted in her *Black, White, and in Color: Essays on American Literature and Culture*, pp. 176–202. Chicago: University of Chicago Press.

Stack, Carol. 1975. *All Our Kin: Strategies for Survival in a Black Community*. New York: Harper.

Star, Susan Leigh. 1983. "Simplification in Scientific Work: An Example From Neuroscience Research." *Social Studies of Science*, 13, pp. 208–226.

—. 2010. "This is Not a Boundary Object: Reflections on the Origin of a Concept." *Science, Technology and Human Values*, 35, pp. 601–617.

Star, Susan Leigh and James Griesemer. 1989. "Institutional Ecology, 'Translations' and Boundary Objects: Amateurs and Professionals in Berkeley's Museum of Vertebrate Zoology, 1907-1939." *Social Studies of Science*, 19, pp. 387–420.

Statistics Korea. 2007. "Population Trends of the World and Korea." Available at http://kostat.go.kr/portal/eng/pressReleases/8/12/index.board?bmode=read&aSeq=273103&pageNo=1&rowNum=10&amSeq=&sTarget=title&sTxt= (accessed 12 January 2018).

Steffen, Will, et al. 2015. "Planetary Dashboard." Global Change: International Geosphere-Biosphere Program. 15 January. Available at: http://www.igbp.net/news/pressreleases/pressreleases/planetarydashboardshowsgreatacceleration inhumanactivitysince1950.5.950c2fa1495db7081eb42.html (accessed 26 September 2017).

Steffen, Will, Wendy Broadgate, Lisa Deutsch, Owen Gaffney, and Cornelia Ludwig. 2015. "The Trajectory of the Anthropocene: The Great Acceleration." *The Anthropocene Review*, 2, n. 1, pp. 81–98. Available at: doi: 10.1177/2053019614564785 (accessed 17 January 2018).

Stengers, Isabelle. 2015. *In Catastrophic Times: Resisting the Coming Barbarism*. Translated by Andrew Goffey. London, UK: Open Humanities Press and Meson Press.

—. 2017. "Autonomy and the Intrusion of Gaia." *South Atlantic Quarterly*, 116, n. 2, pp. 381–400.

Strathern, Marilyn. 1988. *The Gender of the Gift: Problems with Women and Problems with Society in Melanesia*. Berkeley, CA: University of California Press.

—. 2013. "Shifting Relations." Emerging Worlds Workshop, University of California at Santa Cruz, 8 February.

Sturm, Circe. 2002. *Blood Politics: Race, Culture, and Identity in the Cherokee Nation of Oklahoma*. Berkeley, CA: University of California Press.

—. 2011. *Becoming Indian: The Struggle over Cherokee Identity in the 21st Century*. Santa Fe, NM: School of Advanced Research Press.

—. 2014. "Race, Sovereignty, and Civil Rights." *Cultural Anthropology*, 29, n. 3, pp. 575–98.

Sufrin, Carolyn. 2017. *Jailcare: Finding the Safety Net for Women behind Bars*. Berkeley, CA: University of California Press.

Sung, Woong Kyu. 2012. "Abortion in South Korea: The Law and the Reality." *International Journal of Law, Policy and the Family*, 26, n. 3, pp. 278–305.

Swanson, Heather. 2017. "Why Anthropologists Need Carrying Capacity: Large-scale Salmon Production, Watershed Change, and the Redistribution of Fish." Paper for the Wenner Gren Workshop on the Patchy Anthropocene. Sintra, Portugal, 8–14 September.

Takeshita, Chikako. 2012. *The Global Biopolitics of the IUD: How Science Constructs Contraceptive Users and Women's Bodies*. Cambridge, MA: The MIT Press.

Taiwan Alliance to Promote Civil Partnership Rights. N.d. "Introduction to the History and Organization of the Taiwan Alliance to Promote Civil Partnership Rights." Available at https://tapcpr.org (accessed 12 January 2018).

Taiwan Childcare Policy Alliance. 2017. "Childcare Policy Alliance Statement of Purpose." Available at: http://cpaboom.blogspot.tw/ (accessed 12 January 2018).

Taiwan Ministry of Health and Welfare, Health Promotion Administration. N.d. "IVF subsidy program for low-income family." Available at https://www.hpa.gov.tw/Pages/Detail.aspx?nodeid=314&pid=436 (accessed 13 January 2018).

Taiwan National Development Council. 2018. "Business Indicators, November 2017." Available at https://www.ndc.gov.tw/en/default.aspx (accessed 12 January 2018).

TallBear, Kim. 2013. *Native American DNA: Tribal Belonging and the False Promise of Genetic Science*. Minneapolis, MN: University of Minnesota Press.

—. 2017. "Beyond the Life/Not-Life Binary: A Feminist-Indigenous Reading of Cryopreservation, Interspecies Thinking, and the New Materialisms." In Joanna Radin and Emma Kowal, eds., *Cryopolitics: Frozen Life in a Melting World*, pp.179–202. Cambridge, MA: MIT Press.

—. 2017. "Moving Beyond Settler (Colonial) Sexualities."
December 6. *Feral Visions: a Decolonial Feminist Podcast from
Liberation Spring*. Available at: https://www.youtube.com/
watch?v=rq0I4TOO-E0 (accessed 9 January 2018).

Taylor, Dorceta. 2014. *Toxic Communities: Environmental
Racism, Industrial Pollution and Residential Mobility*. New
York: New York University Press.

Taylor, Keeanga-Yamahtta. 2016. *From #BlackLivesMatter to Black
Liberation*. Chicago IL: Haymarket Press.

Thomas, Sheree Renee. 2000. *Dark Matter: A Century of
Speculative Fiction from the African Diaspora*. New York:
Warner Books.

—. 2004. *Dark Matter: Reading the Bones*. New York: Warner
Books.

Thompson, Charis. 2007. *Making Parents: The Ontological
Choreography of Reproductive Technologies*. Cambridge, MA:
MIT Press.

—. 2013. *Good Science: The Ethical Choreography of Stem Cell
Research*. Cambridge MA: MIT Press.

Thrush, Glenn. 2017. "Congress Urges President to Denounce
Hate Groups." *The New York Times*, 13 September. Available
at: https://www.nytimes.com/2017/09/12/us/congress-
trump-hate-groups-charlottesville.html (accessed 2 January
2018).

Thrush, Glenn and Maggie Haberman. 2017. "Giving White
Nationalists an Unequivocal Boost." *The New York Times*, 16
August, pp. A1,12.

Todd, Zoe. 2014. "Fish Pluralities: Human-Animal Engagement
and Sites of Engagement in Paulatuuq, Arctic Canada."
Études/Inuit Studies, 38, no. 1–2, pp. 217–38.

—. 2016. "An Indigenous Feminist's Take On The Ontological
Turn: 'Ontology' Is Just Another Word For Colonialism."
Journal of Historical Sociology 29, pp. 4–22. Available at:
http://onlinelibrary.wiley.com/doi/10.1111/johs.12124/
epdf (accessed 17 January 2018).

—. 2016. "Relationships." In Theorizing the Contemporary,
Cultural Anthropology website, 21 January. Available at:
https://culanth.org/fieldsights/799-relationships (accessed
26 September 2017).

Trinidad, Osteria. 2015. "Singlehood as a Lifestyle in Asia." In
Stella Quah, ed., *Routledge Handbook of Families in Asia*, pp.
93–110. Oxford, UK: Routledge.

Tsing, Anna L. 1993. *In the Realm of the Diamond Queen: Marginality in an Out-of-the-Way Place*. Princeton, NJ: Princeton University Press.>

—. 2004. *Friction: An Ethnography of Global Connection*. Princeton, NJ: Princeton University Press.

—. 2015. *The Mushroom at the End of the World: On the Possibility of Life in Capitalist Ruins*. Princeton, NJ: Princeton University Press.

—. 2016. "Earth Stalked by Man." *Cambridge Journal of Anthropology*, 34, no. 1, pp. 2–16.

—. n.d. "Mushrooms as Companion Species." Available at: http://tsingmushrooms.blogspot.com/ (accessed 21 December 2017).

Tsing, Anna, Heather Swanson, Elaine Gan, and Nils Bubandt, eds. 2017. *Arts of Living on a Damaged Planet: Monsters and Ghosts of the Anthropocene*. Minneapolis, MN: University of Minnesota Press.

Tuck, Eve, Mistinguette Smith, Allison Guess, Tavia Benjamin, and Brian K. Jones. 2014. "Geotheorizing Black/Land: Contestations and Contingent Collaborations." *Departures in Critical Qualitative Research*, 3, n. 1, pp. 52–74.

Tuck, Eve, and K. Wayne Yang. 2013. "R-Words: Refusing Research." In Django Paris and Maisha T. Winn, eds., *Humanizing Research: Decolonizing Qualitative Inquiry with Youth and Communities*, pp. 223–48. Thousand Oaks, CA: Sage.

Turner, Jenny. 2017. "Life with Ms Cayenne Pepper." *London Review of Books*, 39, n. 11, pp. 23–27.

Ueno, Chizuko. 2007. おひとりさまの老後 *(The Aging Life for a Single Woman)*. Tokyo: Houken Corp. (In Japanese: Ueno, Chizuko. 2007. *Ohitorisama no Rogo*. Tokyo: Houken Corp.)

—. 2009. 男おひとりさま道. *(Men's Ways to be Single)*. Tokyo: Houken Corp. (In Japanese: Ueno, Chizuko. 2009. *Otoko ohitori-sama-dō*. Tokyo: Houken Corp.)

UNEP. 2009. "Global Monitoring Report." UNEP/POPS/ COP.4/33. Geneva. Available at: http://chm.pops.int/ Portals/0/Repository/COP4/UNEP-POPS-COP.4-33.English.PDF (accessed 15 January 2018).

United Nations. 2015. "World Population Prospects: Key Findings and Advance Tables, 2015 Revision." Population Division of the Department of Economic and Social Affairs. Available at: http://esa.un.org/unpd/wpp/Publications/Files/Key_Findings_WPP_2015.pdf (accessed 4 August 2016)

—. 2016. "244 Million International Migrants Living Abroad Worldwide, New UN Statistics Reveal." *UN Sustainable Development Goals.* Available at: http://www.un.org/sustainabledevelopment/blog/2016/01/244-million-international-migrants-living-abroad-worldwide-new-un-statistics-reveal/ (accessed 3 January 2018).

United Nations Refugee Agency. 2017. "Figures at a Glance." Available at: http://www.unhcr.org/en-us/figures-at-a-glance.html (accessed 20 December 2017).

US Environmental Protection Agency [USEPA]. 2015. "Great Lakes Facts and Figures." Overviews and Factsheets. US EPA. September 18. Available at: https://www.epa.gov/great-lakes/great-lakes-facts-and-figures (accessed 15 January 2018).

Vandenberg, Laura N., Theo Colborn, Tyrone B. Hayes, Jerrold J. Heindel, David R. Jacobs, Duk-Hee Lee, Toshi Shioda, et al. 2012. "Hormones and Endocrine-Disrupting Chemicals: Low-Dose Effects and Nonmonotonic Dose Responses." *Endocrine Reviews*, 33, n. 3, pp. 378–455. Available at: https://doi.org/10.1210/er.2011-1050 (accessed 15 January 2018).

Van Dooren, Thom. 2014. *Flight Ways: Life and Loss at the Edge of Extinction.* New York: Columbia University Press.

van Kammen, Jessica and Nelly Oudshoorn. 2002. "Gender and Risk Assessment in Contraceptive Technologies." *Sociology of Health and Illness*, 24, n. 4, pp. 436–461.

Verran, Helen Watson. 2001. *Science and an African Logic.* Chicago, IL: University of Chicago Press.

Verran, Helen Watson and David Turnbull. 1995. "Science and Other Indigenous Knowledge Systems." In Sheila Jasanoff, Gerlad E. Markle, James C. Petersen, and Trevor Pinch (eds.), *Handbook of Science and Technology Studies*, pp. 115–139. Thousand Oaks, CA: Sage.

Vizenor, Gerald Robert. 2000. *Fugitive Poses: Native American Indian Scenes of Absence and Presence.* Lincoln, KS: University of Nebraska Press.

Voyles, Traci Brynne. 2015. *Wastelanding: Legacies of Uranium Mining in Navajo Country*. Minneapolis, MN: University of Minnesota Press.

Vrijheid, Martine. 2014. "The Exposome: A New Paradigm to Study the Impact of Environment on Health." *Thorax*, 69 n. 9, pp. 876–78. Available at: https://doi.org/10.1136/thoraxjnl-2013-204949 (accessed 15 January 2018).

Vrijheid, Martine, Rémy Slama, Oliver Robinson, Leda Chatzi, Muireann Coen, Peter van den Hazel, Cathrine Thomsen, et al. 2014. "The Human Early-Life Exposome (HELIX): Project Rationale and Design." *Environmental Health Perspectives*, 122, n. 6, pp. 535–44. Available at: https://doi.org/10.1289/ehp.1307204 (accessed 15 January 2018).

Wacquant, Loïc. 2004. *Deadly Symbiosis: Race and the Rise of Neoliberal Penalty*. Cambridge, UK: Polity.

Waggoner, Miranda R. and Uller, Tobias. 2015. "Epigenetic Determinism in Science and Society." *New Genetics and Society*, 34, n. 2, pp. 17–195.

Wahlberg, Ayo and Tine Gammeltoft, eds. 2018. *Selective Reproduction in the 21st Century*. London, UK: Palgrave Macmillan.

Waldby, Catherine. 2015. "'Banking time': Egg-freezing and the Negotiation of Future Fertility." *Culture, Health & Sexuality*, 17, n. 4, pp. 470–482.

Ware, Cellestine. 1970. *Woman Power: The Movement for Women's Liberation*. New York: Tower Publications.

Watt-Coultier, Sheila. 2015. *The Right to Be Cold*. Toronto, Ontario, Canada: Allen Lane.

Webster, Andy. 2017. "The Untold Tales of Armistead Maupin." *The New York Times*, 29 September: C6.

Wee, Sui-Lee. 2017. "After One-Child Policy, Outrage at China's Offer to Remove IUDs." *The New York Times*, 7 January. Available at: https://www.nytimes.com/2017/01/07/world/asia/after-one-child-policy-outrage-at-chinas-offer-to-remove-iuds.html (accessed 1 January 2018).

Weheliye, Alexander, G. 2014. *Habeas Viscus: Racializing Assemblages, Biopolitics, and Black Feminist Theories of the Human*. Durham, NC: Duke University Press.

Weis, Tony. 2013. *The Ecological Hoofprint: the Global Burden of Industrial Livestock*. London, UK: Zed Books.

Weisiger, Marsha L. 2011. *Dreaming of Sheep in Navajo Country*. Seattle, WA: University of Washington Press.

Whitmee, Sarah, et al. 2015. "Safeguarding Human Health in the Anthropocene Epoch: Report of the Rockefeller Foundation-Lancet Commission on Planetary Health." *Lancet*, 386, n. 10007, 14 November, pp. 1973–2028. Available at: http://www.thelancet.com/journals/lancet/article/PIIS0140-6736(15)60901-1/fulltext (accessed 15 January 2018).

Whyte, Kyle P. 2017. "Indigenous Climate Change Studies: Indigenizing Futures, Decolonizing the Anthropocene." *English Language Notes*, 55, n. 1–2, pp. 153–62.

—. 2017. "Is It Colonial Deja Vu? Indigenous Peoples and Climate Injustice." In Joni Adamson and Michael Davis, eds., *Humanities for the Environment: Integrating Knowledges, Forging New Constellations of Practice*, pp. 88–104. London: Routledge.

—. 2017. "Our Ancestors' Dystopia Now: Indigenous Conservation and the Anthropocene." In Ursula Heise, Jon Christensen, and Michelle Niemann, eds., *Routledge Companion to the Environmental Humanities*, pp. 206–215. New York and London: Routledge.

—. Forthcoming. "What Do Indigenous Knowledges Do for Indigenous Peoples?" In Melissa K. Nelson and Dan Shilling, eds., *Keepers of the Green World: Traditional Ecological Knowledge and Sustainability*. Cambridge, UK: Cambridge University Press. Abstract available at SSRN: https://ssrn.com/abstract=2612715 (accessed 18 January 2018).

Wikipedia. 2012. "List of Countries by Carbon Dioxide Emissions per Capita." Available at: https://en.wikipedia.org/wiki/List_of_countries_by_carbon_dioxide_emissions_per_capita (accessed 11 August 2016).

Willey, Angela. 2016. *Undoing Monogamy: The Politics of Science and the Possibilities of Biology*. Durham and London: Duke University Press.

Williams, Raymond. 1976. *Keywords: A Vocabulary of Culture and Society*. London, UK: Flamingo-Fontana/Croom Helm.

Wilson, Kalpana. 2015. "The 'New' Global Population Control Policies: Fueling India's Sterilization Atrocities." *Different Takes*, 87 (Winter): Population and Development Program, Hampshire College. Available at: https://sites.hampshire.edu/popdev/different-takes/ (accessed 9 January 2018).

Wilson, Kristin J. 2014. *Not Trying: Infertility, Childlessness and Ambivalence*. Nashville, TN: Vanderbilt University Press.

Winant, Howard. 2014. "The Dark Matter: Race and Racism in the 21st Century." *Critical Sociology* 41, n. 2, pp. 313–324.

Wing, Nick. 2016. "Our Bail System Is Leaving Innocent People To Die In Jail Because They're Poor." *Justice Policy Institute*, 14 July. Available at http://www.justicepolicy.org/news/10585 (accessed 3 January 2018).

Wolfe, Cary, ed. 2003. *Zootologies: The Question of the Animal*. Minneapolis: University of Minnesota Press.

World Atlas. 2017. "Countries with the Most Dogs." Available at: https://www.worldatlas.com/articles/countries-with-the-most-dogs-worldwide.html (accessed 21 December 2017).

World Health Organization. 2012. "State of the Science of Endocrine Disrupting Chemicals." Available at: http://www.who.int/ceh/publications/endocrine/en/ (accessed 15 January 2018).

World Population History. 2016. Interactive map. Available at: http://worldpopulationhistory.org/map/1/mercator/1/0/25/ (accessed 10 August 2016).

Wu, Chia-Ling. 2012. "IVF Policy and Global/Local Politics: The Making of Multiple-Embryo Transfer Regulation in Taiwan." *Social Science and Medicine*, 75, n. 4, pp. 725–732.

—. 2017. "From Single Motherhood to Queer Reproduction: Access Politics of Assisted Conception in Taiwan." In Angela Leung and Izumi Nakayama, eds., *Gender and Health in Modern East Asia*, pp. 92–114. Hong Kong: Hong Kong University Press.

Wu, Ming-Yi. 2015. *The Man with Compound Eyes: A Novel*. London: Vintage.

Wynes, Seth and Kimberly Nicholas. 2017. "The Climate Mitigation Gap." *Environmental Research Letters*, 12, n. 7, (12 July). Available at: http://iopscience.iop.org/article/10.1088/1748-9326/aa7541/meta. (accessed 25 September 2017).

Wynter, Sylvia. 1984. "The Ceremony Must Be Found: After Humanism." *Boundary* 2, 12, n.3, pp. 19–70.

—. 2003. "Unsettling the Coloniality of Being/Power/Truth/Freedom: Towards the Human, After Man, Its Overrepresentation—An Argument." *CR: The New Centennial Review*, 3, n. 3, pp. 257–337.

Yamada, Masahiro. 1999. パラサイト・シングルの時代 [*The Age of Parasite Singles*]. Tokyo: Chikumashobo Ltd. (In Japanese: Yamada, Masahiro. 1999. *Parasaito shinguru no jidai*. Tokyo: Kabushiki Kaisha Chikuma Shobō.)

—. 2013. なぜ日本は若者に冷酷なのか: そして下降移動社会が到来する [*Why is Japan so Cruel to the Young? The Coming of Downwardly Mobile Society*]. Tokyo: Toyo Keizai Inc. (In Japanese: Yamada, Masahiro. 2013. *Naze Nihon wa waka-mono ni reikokuna no ka: Soshite kakō idō shakai ga tōrai suru*. Tokyo: Kabushiki-gaisha Tōyō Keizai Shinpōsha.)

Yanow, Dvora and Peregrine Schwartz-Shea. 2006. *Interpretation and Method: Empirical Research Methods and the Interpretive Turn*. New York: Routledge.

Yip, Paul. 2017. "Hong Kong Should Make the Best of Being a Low-Fertility Society." *South China Morning Post*, 27 July. Available at: http://www.scmp.com/comment/insight-opinion/article/2103608/hong-kong-should-make-best-being-low-fertility-society (accessed 1 January 2018).

Yong, Ed. 2017. "The Desirability of Storytellers." *The Atlantic*, 5 December. Available at: https://www.theatlantic.com/science/archive/2017/12/the-origins-of-storytelling/547502/ (accessed 20 December 2017).

—. 2018. "When Humans War, Animals Die." *The Atlantic*, 10 January. Available at: https://www.theatlantic.com/science/archive/2018/01/when-humans-war-animals-die/549902/?utm_source=fbb (accessed 12 January 2018).

Yoshikawa, Hiroshi. 2016. 人口と日本経済──長寿、イノベーション、経済成長 [*Population and Japanese Economy—Longevity, Innovation and Economic Growth*]. Tokyo: Chuokoron-Shinsha. (In Japanese: *Jinkou to Nihon no keizai—Chōju, inobēshon, keizai seichō*. Tokyo: Chuokoron-Shinsha.)

Young, Damon. 2017. "Do White People Have Cousins?" *The Root/VSB*, 22 November. Available at: https://verysmartbrothas.theroot.com/do-white-people-have-cousins-1820685828 (accessed 18 January 2018).

Zahara, Alex. 2016. "Boundaries of the Human in the Age of the Life Sciences." Sites at Penn State/Events, 14 July. Available at: http://sites.psu.edu/iahboundaries/alex-zahara/ (accessed 18 January 2018).

Zak, Dank. 2015. "A Ground Zero Forgotten." *The Washington Post*, 27 November. Available at: http://www.washingtonpost.com/sf/national/2015/11/27/a-ground-zero-forgotten/?utm_term=.09f88f6652d9 (accessed 3 January 2018).

Zika Social Science Network (ZSSN). 2017. "ZSSN Website." Available at: https://www.zssn.org/about/ (accessed 10 January 2018).

Zimmerman, Kristen and Vera Miao. 2009. *Fertile Ground: Women Organizing at the Intersection of Environmental Justice and Reproductive Justice*. Oakland CA: Movement Strategy Center. Available at: http://www.racialequitytools.org/resourcefiles/zimmerman.pdf (accessed 29 December 2017).

Zurn, Perry and Andrew Dilts. 2016. *Active Intolerance: Michel Foucault, the Prisons Information Group, and the Future of Abolition*. New York: Palgrave MacMillan.

Also available from Prickly Paradigm Press:

continued

continued